P9-CCQ-607

AMERICAN IMMIGRATION:

Our History, Our Stories

AMERICAN IMMIGRATION:

Our History, Our Stories

KATHLEEN KRULL

HARPER

An Imprint of HarperCollinsPublishers

Library of Congress Control Number: TK
ISBN 978-0-06-238113-2
Typography by TK
20 21 22 23 24   XXXXXX   10 9 8 7 6 5 4 3 2 1
❖
First Edition

to all the immigrants in my life

CONTENTS

★ ★ ★

INTRODUCTION

★ ★ ★

No Place Like America

America is one very popular country. For centuries, ever since its start as a small collection of English colonies, it has absorbed people from every corner of the globe. Our country is made up of those people.

We call them immigrants. Immigration is one of the great, unique themes of American history. Today, American immigrants number more than forty million—America has more immigrants than any other country in the world. Among people moving from another country in recent years, approximately one-fifth of them immigrated here—an exceptionally diverse population, representing just about every country in the world.

And all these newcomers have stories. Many have

Immigrants at Ellis Island

escaped cruel, nightmarish situations in other countries. Others are in search of the American dream, a fresh beginning in a land where all things seem possible. People love America for its spectacular natural resources, its endless opportunities to make a better life. Perhaps most of all, families come here to provide a better future for their children, to put down roots and thrive on our freedoms. To them, America may not be perfect, but it represents an improvement over the past.

Immigration is all about the people. They come here by choice, often going to extraordinary lengths to do so. Some are famous—people like Alexander Hamilton,

Annie Moore, Albert Einstein, to name a few—while most of them are not.

> "Once I thought to write a *history* of the immigrants in America. Then I discovered that the immigrants *were* American history."
>
> —Oscar Handlin, *considered the father of American immigration history*

★ WHAT UNITES US ★

One striking fact about the United States is that we are united not by ethnicity, as are most other countries. And it's not religion or language or what we look like that we have in common, either. Nor is it ancient history that shapes us.

Instead, it's our shared values. These values are based on our revolutionary founding documents, the Declaration of Independence and the United States Constitution. It's our idea of democracy—a system of government ruled by and for all kinds of people—that throughout our past made America a magnet and kept it united.

Our Founders who wrote those documents drew their ideas from the Age of Enlightenment (approximately 1688 to 1789). This was a movement in Europe toward using the scientific method instead of superstition to solve problems. The Founders were in love with Enlightenment ideas—liberty, tolerance, the use of reason, progress, separation of church and state.

> "Muslims are Americans, Americans are Muslims. Muslims participate in the well-being of this country as American citizens. We are proud American citizens. It's the values that brought us here, not our religion. . . . This country is not strong because of its economic power or military power. This country is strong because of its values."
>
> —*Khizr Khan, father of American army captain killed during the Iraq War*

A special favorite was the Enlightenment resistance to an absolute monarchy, with kings and rich aristocrats telling all the other people what to do. Impatient to separate from the monarchy of Great Britain, our Founders used Enlightenment ideals to fuel their hopes and dreams for a new country.

That's why they came up with our unifying, all-important documents. First, in 1776, was the bold Declaration of Independence (eight of whose fifty-five signers were born in another country). Then, after the Revolutionary War—and not without a *lot* of debate—the Founders spelled out how the new country was to work with all the provisions in the Constitution (1787), and the Bill of Rights (1791).

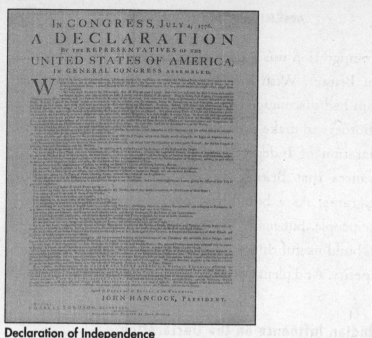

Declaration of Independence

The Constitution

Immigration was a sticking point with our nemesis, Great Britain. With the Royal Proclamation of 1763, Britain had discouraged newcomers, wanting to restrict our borders to make the colonies easier to control. The Declaration of Independence had as one of its main grievances that Britain was imposing limits on new immigrants. As a brand-new country, we needed not fewer people, but *more*. We needed people to work the land, build useful things, mine natural resources, create prosperity. And plenty of people wanted to come.

★ Indian Influence on the Declaration of Independence

A man of his time, Ben Franklin alternated between dismissal of Indians and respect for them. He did admire the Iroquois Confederacy, which united the Oneida, Mohawk, Cayuga, Seneca, Onondaga, and Tuscarora nations in a democracy based on laws in common. Their centuries-old constitution, known as the Great Law of Peace, struck Franklin as a model for what the colonies could do. As Congress debated the Declaration, they invited some twenty Iroquois Confederacy chiefs to act as advisers. Ultimately, of course, the document excluded Indians (as well as African Americans), a contradiction to American ideals right from the start, reflecting the racism embedded in our society.

The place that America would become was foreseen in these three documents. The Founders anticipated our diversity of cultural, religious, and political beliefs. So they made plans for us to try to live together, without the deadly religious and ethnic conflicts ravaging other parts of the world. Unlike many countries that have restrictions on who they let in and how many, we have a long and overall successful history of taking in new people and integrating them.

★ The Enlightenment

"It doesn't take much to rip off the politeness and the accommodation that really keeps diverse peoples working and living together. . . . I think we are living at a time when there is a deliberate assault on truth and reason. I think the Enlightenment was a pretty good deal, and it helped to provide the intellectual and philosophical underpinnings of our Founders. And I still believe that we are the greatest man-made invention in the history of the world, and we can't give up on that. And we can't get discouraged. And we have to figure out ways we are going to keep going."
—*Former Secretary of State Hillary Clinton, 2017*

In designing our documents, the Founders showed that they were well aware of what they were doing:

limiting the powers of government for the purpose of reducing conflict and preserving people's individual freedom.

As Founder James Madison stressed in 1788: "In a free government the security for civil rights must be the same as that for religious rights. It consists in the one case in the multiplicity of interests, and in the other in the multiplicity of sects"—or various branches of religions. The key word is *multiplicity*—America had to be elastic enough to hold people from many places, with different interests and different religions.

What Do the Founding Documents Actually Say About Immigrants?

Not much. The word *immigrant* appears nowhere in the documents. The only limitation mentioned is that the president and vice president have to be "natural-born citizens," meaning born in the United States. But immigrants are eligible for all other political offices.

Even the Founders themselves didn't agree on the topic of immigration. But the prevailing attitude was encouraging—that's how the new country would grow and thrive. It was already being proven that those willing to take a chance in a new land were a self-selected group with all kinds of useful qualities—the motivation to succeed, the willingness to take risks, a strong work ethic, and more.

★ How the Founders Helped

"Our forefathers understood the very nature and need for our nation to replenish itself through future immigration. It is at the very foundation of our national DNA. It is who we are. We are, and hopefully always will be, a nation of immigrants. We are told by our founders that we must endeavor to encourage migration to our exceptional nation. That is part and parcel of . . . our Declaration of Independence."

—*Robert Gittelson, President of Conservatives for Comprehensive Immigration Reform, 2013*

★ THE GOLDEN DOOR ★

The Statue of Liberty, installed in New York Harbor in 1886, remains a symbol all over the world for a fresh start. Inscribed on it several years afterward are some of the most famous words ever, a cheer for the "golden door" that America represented:

New York: An ocean steamer passing the Statue of Liberty

"Give me your tired, your poor,
Your huddled masses yearning to breathe free,
The wretched refuse of your teeming shore.
Send these, the homeless, tempest-tost to me,
I lift my lamp beside the golden door!"

★ Immigrant Story—Emma Lazarus

Emma Lazarus wrote "The New Colossus," the poem engraved on a plaque on the Statue of Liberty. Her family could trace its ancestry to some of the first Jewish settlers in America, those fleeing Spain and Portugal in the 1700s. She started publishing her poetry when she was seventeen, and she went on to become one of the first successful Jewish American authors. Her most memorable poem expresses an intense compassion for newcomers and is treasured by many, including those who today use it as a rallying cry for immigrants' rights.

Emma Lazarus

America had such welcoming, open arms that passports—the legal documents required for international travel—were not needed to come here until relatively recently, in 1941, during the tumult of World War II. With some exceptions that did begin cropping up, all were invited.

Immigrants came in waves, waves that sometimes reached tsunami level.

Those who have surfed the waves to come here from every continent and every country have contributed to and enriched all aspects of American life. They brought their muscles, talents, hearts, and brains. They built our cities, our railroads, and our highways. They mined coal and iron, produced textiles in factories, cultivated our farmlands and grew food for the nation to eat. They fought to defend their new country in every branch of the American military.

> "This land is your land, this land is my land . . . This land was made for you and me."
> —*musician Woody Guthrie, whose ancestors were from all over Europe, 1940*

Immigrants are a bit of a gift that keeps on giving. They oftentimes arrive when they're young, during their most productive working years, and they tend to fill crucial niches in the economy, not so much competing with American workers as complementing them. Many come here with valuable skill sets, and most bring a strong desire to work. Their children, pushed by parents not wanting them to waste the gift of a new life, tend to reach high levels of achievement.

Innovators and inventors have flocked here, bringing new perspectives, eager to problem solve. More than forty percent of the richest companies in America—such as Google, eBay, Apple, Home Depot, McDonald's, and more—were founded by immigrants or the children of immigrants.

★ CONTROVERSY ★

And yet . . . immigration continues to provoke major tension in America: a push-pull sensation. From the very beginning, we've engaged in debate—a "we want you" attitude versus "we don't want you."

Is immigration America's greatest strength, or a source of its ruin? Are we a "melting pot," or a "dumping ground"? Should we show compassion, or protect ourselves? Are we a multicultural nation, strengthened by our diversity? Or do new people make America less . . . American?

Pro Immigration

"[Immigrants are] a source of national wealth and strength."

—*President Abraham Lincoln, 1863, asking Congress to encourage immigration*

"One of the reasons why America is such a diverse and inclusive nation is because we're a nation of immigrants. Our Founders conceived of this country as a refuge for the world. And for more than two centuries, welcoming wave after wave of immigrants has kept us youthful and dynamic and entrepreneurial. It has shaped our character, and it has made us stronger."

—*President Barack Obama, 2016*

★ Against Immigration

"To admit foreigners indiscriminately to the rights of citizens, the moment they put foot in our country . . . would be nothing less than to admit the Grecian horse into the citadel of our liberty

Alexander Hamilton

and sovereignty"—that is, something threatening.

—*Founder Alexander Hamilton (an immigrant), 1802*

"Those who come hither are generally of the most ignorant stupid sort of their own nation."

—*Founder Ben Franklin, 1753*

We appreciate immigrants' food—from kimchi to tacos. We adopt some of their customs (setting off fireworks, which originated in China), celebrate some of their holidays (wearing Irish green on Saint Patrick's Day), and we rely on their labor, especially in the most physically demanding jobs, like picking crops and cleaning houses. We love immigrant success stories, like six-year-old Sergey Brin immigrating from the Soviet Union and going on to found Google.

But many also feel spasms of fear about immigrants—changing America, using up our resources, potentially being criminals. Or immigrants taking our jobs, not paying taxes, or draining our economy.

The immigration laws we have passed crisscross the whole range of opinions, from fear to welcome. Our presidents have disagreed with each other throughout history—sometimes they even disagree with themselves, expressing contradictory opinions.

Thoughts about this topic are like a mirror held up to society's latest worries. Immigrants can make a handy target for fears about whatever is going on at the time.

Newcomers are by definition new, not always understood, and people often fear what they don't understand. One word for this fear is nativism. Something in human nature often resents those who are other than us—"foreigners," people other than "natives." Racism is a strong undercurrent in American history, and it has often spurred nativism. For some, being an American means being a white Protestant who speaks English—others don't quite qualify.

Just about every wave of immigrants has been protested—sometimes viciously—by those who claim these newbies just won't assimilate, or do what it takes to become "American."

There's a bit of irony that goes with nativism : immigrants who have lived here for a while tend to get amnesia about their own reasons for moving here and the struggle it took to uproot themselves and make the journey. Some look down on the newcomers. With all the various waves, this intolerance phenomenon happens over and over.

Irony pops up often in immigration history.

★ NOT ALL OF US ARE IMMIGRANTS ★

To state that we are all immigrants, or descended from immigrants, is not precisely true. It's more complicated, as with everything else in American history.

The indigenous people who were here first are one major exception—the American Indian nations of the various regions of the continent, speaking some 1,200 separate languages. Indians were self-sufficient, self-ruled caretakers of the land. They hunted, built things, bought and sold goods, formed alliances, and above all

American Indians

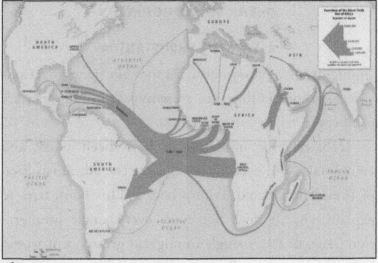

Africa map

farmed. In their expertise with plants and herbs, they were the greatest farmers and doctors of their time, with knowledge centuries ahead of what Europeans believed.

Millions of enslaved people forced to come here from Africa—from many different countries, with their own cultures and languages—and their descendants are the other exception. If we define "immigrant" as a person who migrates from, or voluntarily leaves, one country to take up residence in another, these two groups don't match the definition.

Of course these two groups have contributed immeasurably to American society—they each deserve a separate book—but for the purposes of this one, we call immigrants those who *wanted* to move here, making a deliberate choice.

★ WHY IT'S IMPORTANT ★

Immigration is messy and hard to make generalizations about without falling into stereotypes. Immigrants are just people, fellow human beings.

Debates over immigration have been noisy and emotional—and even more so since the administration of President Donald Trump began. This book tries to explain why. It does not cover every single immigration issue, or every single immigrant group, or it would be too heavy to lift. But it tries to provide a context for discussions and debates today, with stories of individual immigrants.

As Senator Edward Kennedy once emphasized, "Immigration is the story of American history." This country is teeming with *millions* of fascinating, high-drama immigrant stories.

It's all about the people.

CHAPTER ONE

★ ⭐ ★

Who Was Here First?

We call it the pre-Columbian period—the time when people were in the Americas before Christopher Columbus or any of the other European explorers showed up. Believe it or not, research is still ongoing about how and when these first people got here.

★ NEW NEWS FROM OLD BONES ★

For many years, we believed America's original inhabitants came here on foot, walking across a land bridge that used to connect Asia and North America some fifteen thousand or more years ago.

Today, scholars are uncovering new information. In 2016, research showed that the corridor between Siberia and Alaska would have been impossible to travel, contradicting the longstanding theory. That would mean that the very first pre-Columbian settlers of America must have traveled either by sea or by hugging the Pacific shoreline.

Then, in 2017, San Diego History Museum scientists were studying shattered mastodon bones that had been found at a site in San Diego, California. The bones had the scars of human activity from 130,700 years ago, they said—some type of human smashing them with a stone hammer, perhaps to get out the marrow to eat. That pushed back the date that humans are thought to have settled North America by 115,000 or so years. This is a major rewrite of the timeline of when humans first arrived in the Americas.

In any case, over all those thousands of years, their descendants gradually migrated east and south. Eventually, two whole continents were populated with indigenous tribal nations speaking some 1,200 languages.

Only a tiny percent of Americans can claim American Indian ancestry. So who is everyone else descended from?

★ BEFORE WE WERE EVEN A COUNTRY ★

We refer to the earliest European arrivals to America as settlers, but of course, America was already settled—by the indigenous people who had been living here for centuries. To claim land for themselves, immigrants had to take it—mostly in violent ways—from the Indians. It is a mistake to think of the Indian nations as being alike—they were different, in languages, traditions, and attitudes toward white newcomers. They responded to the invasion in many different ways, but always, the odds were against them.

By the time of the Revolutionary War, the rapidly growing American population outnumbered Indians by twenty to one, making colonists ever bolder about taking over more land. The British had more favorable policies toward Indians, and during the war most tribes sided with the British or stayed neutral; only a small minority backed the new colonists' side. Had the British won the war, in fact, it's possible the Indians would have fared better over the years than they did with the new Americans. But the Americans won, and began official policies of forcibly removing Indians from their lands and moving them to reservations.

Fifteen million Indians were here when Christopher Columbus arrived in 1492. By 1900, disease and government cruelty had reduced that number to 250,000.

The Original Americans

"Our nation was born in genocide when it embraced the doctrine that the original American, the Indian, was an inferior race. Even before there were large numbers of Negroes on our shores, the scar of racial hatred had already disfigured colonial society. From the sixteenth century forward, blood flowed in battles of racial supremacy." —*Dr. Martin Luther King, Jr.*

By the 1500s, the first Europeans, led by the Spanish and the French, had begun establishing settlements in what would become the United States. Leaving their Old World, they were lured by all the promises of what they thought of as the New World—riches, freedom, adventure.

In 1565, St. Augustine, Florida, our oldest city, was founded by the Spanish. Thanks to a combination of yearly hurricanes, poor management, and disease-bearing

Plan of the Town of St. Augustine, the capital of East Florida, 1777

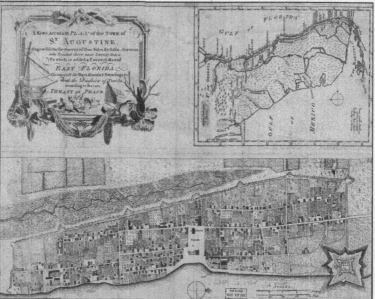

mosquitoes, Spain sent few settlers to Florida. It seemed like an uninhabitable swamp. They were more likely to build forts in present-day New Mexico and California, where Spanish settlers founded Los Angeles in 1781.

French expeditions established footholds on the Saint Lawrence River, Mississippi River, and Gulf Coast. Trading posts, forts, and cities went up throughout Louisiana, notably the great, multicultural city of New Orleans, founded in 1718. The city of Detroit, founded in 1701, became the third-largest settlement in New France.

★ NEW ENGLAND ★

Newcomers from England followed. The English were by far the largest group of early arrivals. The two great draws were freedom of religion and cheap, fertile land. Over 90 percent of these early immigrants became farmers.

Success in the New World was by no means a given. One settlement, established in 1587 in Dare County, North Carolina, simply disappeared—the mysterious Lost Colony of Roanoke.

In 1607, the English succeeded in founding their first permanent settlement at Jamestown in the Virginia Colony.

This was a commercial venture, designed to make money. Investors from a company in London expected to reap sweet rewards from a settlement at Jamestown. But

Jamestown Settlement fort

the arrivals were mostly gentlemen, utterly inept at dealing with the challenges of their new wilderness locale. Eight out of ten of them died from disease and starvation within the first few months.

More ships arrived in 1608, bearing skilled workers from Germany, Poland, and Slovakia.

Jamestown struggled along, with more downs than ups, but it continued to grow. Then, after the whole settlement burned down during a rebellion against the unpopular local governor, the town was moved and renamed Williamsburg in 1699.

Meanwhile, the *Mayflower* arrived in 1620 with 102 English Pilgrims, many of them children, taking root near Plymouth, Massachusetts. This was also a for-profit venture, but with a twist—religion. The Pilgrims were members of a strict branch of Protestantism that had religious differences with the Church of England, the official Anglican religion of Great Britain. Pilgrims wanted their congregations to be separate. To separate, they had to go somewhere else—a pilgrim being someone who takes a long journey to a foreign land for religious reasons.

Nearby Netherlands welcomed them, but the Pilgrims wanted to be even more separate. So they arranged with a group of London merchants to finance a new colony of their own in North America. The investors were hoping the settlers would discover precious metals.

Half of these Pilgrims would die in the first year, sometimes two or three in one day during the winter of the "great sickness."

★ Immigrant Stories—Children of the Mayflower

The brave children who sailed aboard the *Mayflower* included:

—**Mary Chilton, age thirteen,** who according to legend was the first one ashore, so excited that she jumped out of the small boat and right onto Plymouth Rock. Both of her parents died the next year. She was given three shares of land, one for herself and one each for her deceased parents. She married a later arrival and had ten children.

The family moved to Boston, where her husband did well as a merchant. Her descendants include President George H. W. Bush and First Lady Lucretia Garfield.

—**Elder Love Brewster, age nine**, with his younger brother, Wrestling. He later married and had four children, became a successful farmer, and helped found the town of Bridgewater, Massachusetts. His descendants number in the thousands.

—**Mary Allerton, age three,** and her older siblings Bartholomew and Remember. Their father, Isaac Allerton, was actively involved in the colony's finances, though eventually banished for corruption. His apprentice was John Hooke, age thirteen, who died during the first winter. Mary lived out her life in Plymouth and married a later arrival, with seven of their children surviving to adulthood, and at least fifty grandchildren. Upon her death at eighty-three, she was the last surviving *Mayflower* passenger.

—**Henry Samson, age sixteen**, traveled as a nephew of another family, along with a one-year-old cousin, Humility Cooper (she survived into her teens and returned to England). His aunt and uncle died in the first winter, but Henry survived to live a long life in Plymouth. He received a generous land grant, married and had nine children, and performed many years of jury duty and other services.

—Elizabeth Tilley, age thirteen, whose entire family died during the first winter. She went on to marry fellow *Mayflower* passenger John Howland, with whom she had ten children, all of whom lived to adulthood, and eighty-eight grandchildren. She outlived her husband by fifteen years. They have millions of living descendants today, including presidents (Franklin D. Roosevelt, George H. W. Bush, and George W. Bush), first ladies (Edith Roosevelt and Barbara Bush), governors (Sarah Palin and Jeb Bush), poets (Ralph Waldo Emerson and Henry Wadsworth Longfellow), and actors (Humphrey Bogart, the Baldwin brothers, and Chevy Chase).

—Resolved White, age five, came with his parents and his brother Peregrine. After his father died, his mother became the only surviving widow out of the many families who died that first winter. She soon remarried a fellow passenger, in the first wedding in the colony. Resolved went on to receive several generous land grants, marry the daughter of a founder of Massachusetts Bay Colony, and be elected surveyor of highways for Marshfield.

—Four indentured servants—Jasper, Ellen, Mary, and Richard More—between the ages of four and eight. They were the only passengers of royal ancestry. But their well-born father had not believed the four children to be his and, during an ugly legal dispute, he arranged for them to be sent to the New World without their mother's knowledge or consent. Three of the More children died during the first winter. But Richard, once his indentureship expired, went on to become a well-known sea captain who helped deliver vital supplies to the colonies. In his fifty years on the seas Richard never lost a ship, nor had any complaints—until Salem church elders accused him of a relationship with another man's wife. He was excommunicated from the church. After repenting in public, he was restored. He died in his eighties, the last surviving male passenger of the *Mayflower.*

—Samuel Eaton, a baby, believed to be the son of the *Mayflower's* carpenter. He was apprenticed at sixteen to John Cooke, a fellow passenger, who helped his father with land surveying. Samuel married and had a total of six children, later moving to Duxbury and then to Middleboro, where he died in his sixties.

—Constance Hopkins, age fourteen, daughter of the only *Mayflower* passenger who had previously been to the New World. Stephen Hopkins's knowledge of the hunting techniques and languages of American Indians was useful to the Pilgrim leadership. He assisted William Bradford, the governor of Plymouth Colony, through 1636.

Constance went on to marry and have twelve children who survived into adulthood, with seventy-two grandchildren.

—**Priscilla Mullins, eighteen,** with her family. All except Priscilla died in the first winter, leaving her the only single woman of marriageable age. She could have her pick of husbands—and it was a captain on the *Mayflower*, John Alden, who went on to serve in a number of important government positions. She and John had ten children and more descendants than any other Pilgrim family. Alden did have a rival for Priscilla's affection—the newly widowed Captain Miles Standish, the colony's military advisor. The triangle is recounted fancifully in "The Courtship of Miles Standish," the poem by Henry Wadsworth Longfellow (one of their descendants).

Once here, the Pilgrims were able to make a treaty with the local Wampanoag Indians whose land they were taking over, keeping themselves safe from attack. Though disease killed half the Pilgrims in the first year, new arrivals kept coming, and by 1627 Plymouth Colony was a stable community of 120. They never did discover gold or silver, but the farming of tobacco turned out to be surprisingly profitable.

★ Mayflower Magic

People like to brag about being descended from the *Mayflower* Pilgrims. And many are, but probably not as many as the 25 percent of the American population that currently believes it. This doesn't add up with other immigration numbers. The actual number of *Mayflower* descendants is unknown.

In 1628 came the founding of the Massachusetts Bay Colony and other settlements among the northern colonies. These settlers were Protestant Puritans—not as strict as the Pilgrims, but wanting to "purify" the Church of England of its "Catholic" practices. They demanded moral purity down to the tiniest detail, with bans against theater, gambling, and festivities, even Christmas. Very unpopular in England, Puritans were so persecuted that they felt compelled to leave for their own safety. As they settled here, they signed a peace-keeping treaty with the local Pokanoket Indians.

Education was essential to Puritans so that everyone could read the Bible for themselves. By the 1670s, all New England colonies except Rhode Island had laws that required children to be literate (not a requirement in the mother country). In 1636 they started our first university, Harvard, in order to train ministers.

Ironically, the Puritans were themselves intolerant of other religious views. Besides Anglicans and Catholics, they looked down on Quakers and Baptists.

In the years leading up to the American Revolution, New Englanders thrived and spread across Massachusetts, then Connecticut, Rhode Island, New Hampshire, upstate New York, the Great Lakes states, and across the Mississippi.

Almost all of these early British expeditions were organized by private citizens, without much government support or input. As settlements became established, they were nearly independent of British trade. They grew or made almost everything they needed—food, crafts, fine goods, ships—leaving the Old World further and further behind.

Goodbye Kings and Queens, Princes and Dukes

One British institution all but abandoned was the aristocracy. The new settlers generally established their own elected governments and courts and were nearly all self-governing and self-supporting within a few years. This pattern became so ingrained that for the next two hundred years, almost all new settlements would have their own government up and running shortly after arrival.

The rapid growth of the New England colonies—approximately nine hundred thousand people by 1790—was due to several factors. People enjoyed an abundant food supply, with a diet high in protein. New England's climate was relatively healthy, with the cold winters killing the mosquitoes and other disease-bearing insects that threatened areas farther south. Their villages were small and far enough apart to lessen the spread of disease. So the birth rate was high and death rate low.

New Englanders prospered. Besides farming, they had shipbuilding, trading, and fishing as sources of income.

America was growing.

CHAPTER 2

★ ★ ★

Women Take
the Lead

Women, often neglected in history books written by men, had a dynamic role in all stages of American immigration.

For a woman to make the journey from the Old World to the New one, leaving behind everything familiar to fight for survival abroad took unimaginable courage. The stakes were high, and their experiences went from one extreme to another—from an early death to a better life, free from Old-World restrictions on their fates and futures.

Francisca Hinestrosa is the first woman immigrant we know by name. She traveled to America from Spain with the 1539 Florida expedition led by Hernando de Soto.

He wouldn't have included a woman on the mission, but Francisca, not wanting to part from her husband, who was a sailor on the ship, came aboard disguised as a man. We know little about her, except that she died two years later in a Chickasaw Indian raid.

During the rest of that century, other women arrived from Spain and Portugal in expeditions to St. Augustine, Florida, and to areas that became Arizona, Colorado, and Texas.

Seventeen English women were among the Roanoke Colony that vanished without a trace. We know next to nothing about any of them, except its most famous member—Virginia Dare, the first child of English parents born in the New World.

The next English women arrived a year after Jamestown was established in 1607—Anne Forrest (married to Thomas Forrest), and her thirteen-year-old maid, Anne Burras. Young Anne's was the first wedding in the new colonies, and her strength inspired the settlement to welcome more women. She, her husband, and their four daughters survived the brutal "starving time" that almost ended Jamestown and lived out their lives in Virginia.

Eager to increase its population, Jamestown was actively recruiting women, and twenty more arrived in

1609, followed by a hundred more the next year.

Most of them were young, poor, adventurous, and already used to a life of hard work. Here they were in such short supply and high demand that they could be picky. They could marry who they wanted to—unlike the marriages arranged by parents in Europe. Eligible men would meet the arriving ships on the shore, looking as presentable as they could. While the women made their decisions, they received food and housing in exchange for doing laundry and other chores.

At first, land for farming was given to them on the same basis as men—a luxury when independent woman landowners were all but nonexistent in the Old World. This policy changed once men realized it was counter-productive. Women in charge of their own land didn't necessarily need husbands—reducing marriages and the much-desired childbirths.

Their labor was desperately needed, inside the home and outside. Homes were little factories, with women producing everything the family needed—clothes, food, candles, soap, and medical care. Their work began at dawn and lasted until the last flickering candle went out. If they could produce more than they needed, they could barter for things to make their lives better. Women were treated with a new respect here.

Women in Jamestown

In 1620 there were eighteen married women aboard the *Mayflower*. Childbirth in the New World was so precarious that all except four women were dead within the year.

★ Immigrant Story—Anne Bradstreet

Well-educated for a woman of her day, Anne Bradstreet was an early Puritan immigrant, arriving from England in 1630. Both her father and husband were later to serve as governors of the Massachusetts Bay Colony. A poet and a scholar, Bradstreet collected books, amassing a library of nine thousand. When not doing housework and taking care of her eight children, she wrote poems about the world around her, with observations about politics, history, medicine, and theology. No one approved of women writing, and it was important for her to downplay her ambitions. Bradstreet was not responsible for her writing becoming public. Her brother-in-law sent her work off to be published. Her first work was published first in London and then in the colonies as *The Tenth Muse, Lately Sprung Up in America* "by a Gentlewoman of those Parts." This made her the first woman to have her writing published in the New World. Frequently criticized, she never neglected her womanly duties—and never stopped writing. Though in poor health all her life, Bradstreet survived until age sixty, when she succumbed to tuberculosis.

Immigrant Story—Anne Hutchinson

Anne Hutchinson arrived in 1634 from England with her husband and fourteen children in search of religious freedom with the Puritan community of Massachusetts Bay Colony. She was a doctor, midwife, and an outspoken religious scholar. She believed that women as well as men deserved a role in the church and had the right to speak and speak freely. The first woman in the colonies to organize others around her beliefs, she hosted

weekly meetings for women and
men. Puritan ministers found her
such a threat that she was tried
and eventually banished from
the colony in 1637. Though ill
and pregnant with her sixteenth
child, she challenged the
sentence's legitimacy, saying,
"I desire to know wherefore I
am banished." The governor

Anne Hutchinson

responded, "The court knows wherefore and
is satisfied." With her family and some of her
supporters, she established the settlement of
Portsmouth in what became Rhode Island. After
her husband's death she moved to Dutch territory,
in what later became the Bronx in New York
City. In 1643, Hutchinson, six of her children,
and other household members were killed by
Siwanoy Indians, who were outraged at their harsh
treatment by the local governor. She remains one
of the most prominent women in early colonial
history and a significant figure in the history of
religious freedom.

Immigrant Story—Margaret Brent

Margaret Brent was the earliest woman we know
who led a group of settlers—coming to Maryland
from England with her siblings and others in 1638,

in search of better lives. As in many countries, the estate of their father (a lord) went to the oldest son and the other children had to fend for themselves. But once she was in America, her aristocratic background helped her get a grant of land, and she became Maryland's first female landowner. She was also the first woman to demand a seat in colonial government, as a representative of others as well as a landowner in her own right. Attending the Maryland General Assembly, she requested a voice in the council, as well as two votes in its proceedings. "I've come to seek a voice in this assembly. And yet because I am a woman, forsooth I must stand idly by and not even have a voice in the framing of your laws." She was refused and left under protest. Despite the intense pressure, she never married; she was one of the few single

Margaret Brent

English women. She made wise investments in land in Virginia, was active in lending money to new settlers and helping to make Maryland more stable, and died a wealthy woman. Today she is seen as a "founding mother" of Maryland.

★ Immigrant Story—Elizabeth Glover

The first printing press in North America was managed by a woman. Elizabeth Glover came from England in 1638 with her husband, a Puritan clergyman, and their five children, plus printing equipment. Reverend Glover died at sea, but his widow made it ashore with the press. Elizabeth had it set up in Cambridge. It was the first printing press in the colonies, printing almanacs and psalms, plus the oath that every man over twenty years of age, and six months a householder, had to swear to in order to become a citizen of the Massachusetts Bay Colony. Later it published the colony's first book, the *Bay Psalm Book*. Elizabeth married Henry Dunster, the first president of the college that would soon be named for another young clergyman, John Harvard. Elizabeth died two years after remarrying. The prestigious name of Harvard protected the press from criticism, which might otherwise have squashed it, making establishment of the printed word in the United States comparatively easy. The printers were free to accept, refuse, and print whatever they wanted without fear of censorship.

⭐ Immigrant Story—Anna Zenger

Women often gravitated to printing and publishing. The first woman to publish a newspaper in America was a German immigrant, Anna Zenger. She took over the *New-York Weekly Journal* for her husband John when he was jailed for criticizing the governor of New York, and then again after John's death in 1746. She continued to publish weekly, with advertisements, and also printed annual almanacs and stationery. She eventually gave control of the printing business to her stepson and moved to a rural area outside of New York City to open a bookstore.

⭐ Immigrant Story—Mary Musgrove

One of the most well-known frontier women is Mary Musgrove, a bilingual woman born to an English trader and a Yamacraw Indian woman. As a wealthy landowner, she supervised Indian traders and established trading posts. In 1733 the governor of the Georgia colony hired her as his interpreter and advisor on the local Indians. She became an important ambassador between Muscogee Creek Indians and the English colonists. When the Spanish attacked Georgia, she bought food for the colonists and hired Indians with her own money to fight off the Spanish attackers.

★ Immigrant Story—Ann Lee

Leader of one of the very few religions started by a woman, Ann Lee came from England to New York in 1774 to escape persecution. She and her followers were known as Shakers because their worship included dancing rituals, shaking and trembling to purge their sins. Lee preached the pursuit of perfection in every area of life, and Shakers were known for simple living, architecture, and furniture. She called for equality of men and women but also the importance of keeping them separate, rejecting marriage. "We [the Shakers] are the people who turned the world upside down," she said. Their stances were unpopular with just about everyone else—as pacifists, they refused to take sides during the American Revolution. Ann was often met with mob violence and grew frail, dying at forty-eight. At their peak, there were six thousand Shakers, but with the lack of new children, the religion all but died out.

As the colonies expanded, many women assumed roles outside their household chores. Some took in laundry or taught children in their towns. Some ventured forth and became farmers in this lush new land, raising and selling fruits and vegetables. Some opened inns to meet the need for overnight stays between towns. Others learned skills—bookkeeping, operating saws, shoeing horses, running slaughterhouses, building furniture. Women were often a town's undertakers.

Until the American Revolution, most doctors were women, in particular midwives, who helped women survive the precariousness of childbirth. In a land that craved children, midwifery was a prestigious job, and some respected midwives delivered as many as three thousand babies.

The New World was still a man's world, and rules and laws still restricted women's lives. But in America, this work in progress, rules were not always enforced, and rigid gender roles from the Old World didn't necessarily apply. These early immigrants had more responsibilities than ever before—and also more power over their own destiny than perhaps women at any time in history up until then.

They faced danger and challenges galore, but the land of freedom was especially freeing for these first women immigrants.

CHAPTER THREE

★ ★ ★

From New England Outward

★ MIDDLE COLONIES ★

The Dutch established settlements along the Hudson River, most notably New York. By 1700, New York City was prospering as a major trading and commercial center. Right from the beginning, it had the most eclectic collection of residents from many different cultures and religions. Tolerance prevailed for the most part, though the Dutch did look down on Lutherans and Quakers.

During the 1680s, Quakers from Britain and other countries traveled to Pennsylvania, Delaware, and western New Jersey. Quakers were another group dissenting from the Church of England—they decreed that all believers (including women) were priests, not just the ordained ministers. They were anti-war and anti-slavery and were seen to be so outside the mainstream that laws were passed to persecute them.

But Germans dominated—between 1710 and 1775 the majority of settlers in the middle colonies were German. Half the Germans headed to farms, especially in the Midwest (with some going to Texas), while the other half became craftsmen in cities.

Ironically, the English and Irish looked down on the Germans as being just too different from themselves and for keeping many of their traditions. Starting a trend of intolerance of newcomers, illustrious Founder Ben Franklin was critical, lumping Germans in with others he considered "swarthy"—dark-skinned—in other words, not "white" enough.

★ Prejudiced Against Germans

"Why should Pennsylvania, founded by the English, become a colony of aliens, who will shortly be so numerous as to Germanize us instead of our Anglifying them, and will never adopt our language or customs, any more than they can acquire our complexion."

—Ben Franklin, 1751

★ THE FRONTIER ★

The colonial frontier—from Pennsylvania to Georgia—was settled from about 1717 to 1775. The new arrivals were mostly settlers fleeing hard times and religious persecution in northern England, Scotland, and northern Ireland.

Starting around 1763, a wave of the Scots-Irish washed over the Appalachian frontier, adding about 10 percent to our population. Escaping the religious restrictions of their governments, they mostly came as married couples or in families.

The Scots-Irish soon became the dominant culture of the Appalachians, from Pennsylvania to Georgia. They were largely Presbyterian, self-sufficient, and generally hostile to American Indians and Catholics, out of prejudice. They loved the very cheap land and their independence.

They kept moving to the southwest, taking over Indian lands of the Mississippi Valley, pushing relentlessly toward the Midwest, Texas, the Rocky Mountains, and the Great Plains. In this they were aided by their hero, Andrew Jackson, who was also of Scots-Irish heritage.

★ President Andrew Jackson

Previous presidents had ignored American Indians whenever possible, leaving settlers to deal with them on their own. President Andrew Jackson from Tennessee created a turning point with his official aggressive policy. Most notoriously, in 1838, when Cherokee Indians refused to voluntarily leave an area where gold had been discovered, he forced them to walk out of their own land to a reservation in present-day Oklahoma. Their journey, during which thousands died, is now known as the Trail of Tears. More than just about

Andrew Jackson

anyone, Jackson spurred the growth of the new country. He played a direct role in acquiring all or part of five more states, opening much of the South to white development and leaving the local Indian nations destitute and without homes.

★ THE SOUTH ★

At first, the Southern colonies proved inhospitable to new people. In the hot, humid climate, settlers had to cope with malaria, yellow fever, and other contagious diseases, as well as skirmishes with American Indians that didn't go well for the newcomers.

Despite all this, a steady flow of new settlers, mostly

from central and southeast England and London, kept up population growth.

Once the settlers began arriving in large numbers, the diseases they brought with them were increasingly fatal to the Indians, who lacked immunity to them. The leading killer was smallpox. By 1630, Indians no longer dominated the initial areas of settlement.

★ Sounds Like Paradise

"It lies in a mild and temperate climate. The woods are full of buffalos, deer, and wild turkeys. . . . The impartial administration of justices hinders the poor from every kind of oppression from the rich and the great."

—William Byrd II, British founder of Richmond, Virginia, 1736

When settlers found out what a profitable cash crop tobacco was, they established plantations to grow it along the Chesapeake Bay in Virginia and Maryland. Initially, the large plantations were generally owned by friends (mostly minor aristocrats) of the British-appointed governors.

Georgia, the most sparsely settled Southern colony, was not the happiest one. In an attempt to rid their own country of criminals, Britain sent its convicts there—about sixty thousand prisoners were transported during the 1700s. Many of these so-called convicts were guilty merely of being very poor and out of work. Serious criminals were generally executed in Britain, but the British government had the counterproductive policy of jailing people in debt (making it impossible for them to repay it). Georgia and other areas were used as a workhouse on a giant scale—people forced to work without wages.

★ SLAVES, NOT IMMIGRANTS ★

As the colonies grew, hundreds of thousands of Africans were being forcibly taken from their homes and transported to the New World against their will. They were put on slave ships and brought to America to work under harsh conditions at other people's homes and plantations across America. Their valuable skills enriched the wealthy landowners—it's impossible to imagine American history without the contributions of African Americans. But in the racist society of the time, they were treated horribly, were not considered human beings, and were not paid for their work.

Some two-thirds of the ancestors of black Americans brought to this country came through the Port of Charleston. Their points of entry were the Sea Islands

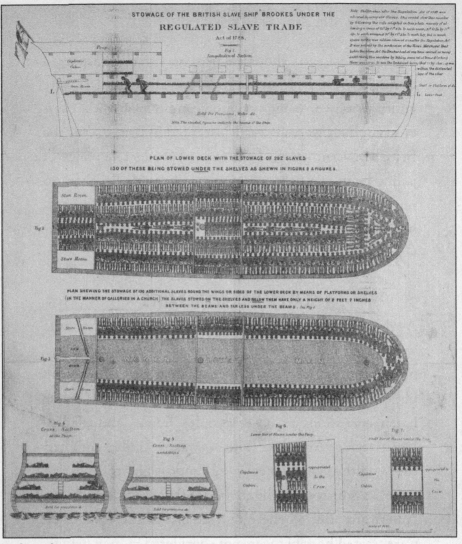

A slave ship

along South Carolina, Georgia, and Florida. The islands developed their own culture and language—Gullah—which continues to the present day.

Much later, toward the end of the 1800s, free Africans

from the Caribbean began to immigrate here by choice. After 1965, the number of immigrants from many countries in Africa would increase.

⭐ Immigrant Story—Claude McKay

Claude McKay was a Jamaican writer and poet who became a leading figure in the Harlem Renaissance, the explosion of African American arts. McKay left Jamaica in 1912 to attend Tuskegee Institute, a historically black college, and became an American citizen in 1940. McKay was shocked by the intense racism he encountered in the South, which inspired his poetry challenging white authority while celebrating Jamaican culture. His work had a major impact on African American authors as well as black intellectuals in the Caribbean, West Africa, and Europe.

⭐ Not "Workers" and Not "Other Immigrants"

"The Atlantic Slave Trade between the 1500s and 1800s brought millions of workers from Africa to the southern United States to work on agricultural plantations."

—from a 2015 McGraw Hill high school textbook until an outcry forced the company to reword the sentence to describe the arrival of Africans in the US as a forced migration and emphasize that their work was done as slave labor

"That's what America is about. A land of dreams and opportunity. There were other immigrants who came here in the bottom of slave ships, worked even longer, even harder for less."

—*Secretary of Housing and Urban Development Ben Carson in 2017, drawing immediate criticism for not recognizing that black "immigrants" were actually forced to come here as slaves*

★ SERVANTS, NOT SLAVES ★

Large numbers of young men and women came here all by themselves from England, and later Germany and Ireland. They were so hungry for work that they made a trade—selling themselves as indentured servants in exchange for passage to the colonies. In their home countries, they signed a legal contract that spelled out their time of service, usually about seven years. Their passage was paid by employers in the colonies who needed help on their farms or in shops.

Indentured servants were provided food, housing, clothing, and training, but did not receive wages for their work. At the end of their term, they were free to do as they wished.

It's been estimated that at least half of the first colonists were indentured servants. By the 1740s the Irish made up nine out of ten indentured servants in some areas.

Indentured servants could be bought and sold like

enslaved people and were subject to brutality. Not all of them entered servitude willingly. Some were children. Their lives were hard, in some ways similar to slavery, but with the all-important difference that freedom was in their sights. Unlike the enslaved, servants were considered legally human. They did not pass their servant status on to their descendants.

As servants earned their freedom (or ran away), slaves replaced them in their jobs. Some servants became landowners, but many remained poor, taking the lowest-paying jobs.

★ The Myth of the Irish "Slaves"

In recent years, rumors have cropped up that the biggest percentage of enslaved people forced to the New World were actually white—people from Ireland sold in the 1640s and '50s. You can see fake photos purporting to be of Irish slaves, but these were actually taken much later (after photography was invented in 1839). Dig deeper and you'll find the myth debunked as an attempt by racists to undermine African American history. It's a way to diminish the horror of slavery—as in, "Even the Irish, we were slaves. At some point, you just have to get over it"—suggesting that present-day white Americans need not feel guilty over what was done in the past. The Irish who came here were indentured servants, and certainly, life for them could be miserable, but it was a completely different category from slavery—it was temporary. The descendants of indentured servants do not face a legacy of racism similar to the one faced by people of African descent.

Fake photos of "Irish slaves."

★ WHAT THE FOUNDERS SAID ★

With the American Revolution in 1775, we declared ourselves a new country. Up until then, those who had been coming here from any other part of the British Empire didn't consider themselves immigrants. They were merely people moving from one end of the Empire to the other.

After 1776, anyone who moved here was officially considered an immigrant.

So what were the "official" attitudes toward immigrants? Mostly they were positive, though objections bubbled up.

Founder Thomas Jefferson explained the situation in detail, speaking in language similar to the Declaration of Independence: "Our ancestors . . . possessed a right, which nature has given to all men, of departing from the country in which chance, not choice, has placed them, of going in quest of new habitations, and of there establishing new societies, under such laws and regulations as, to them, shall seem most likely to promote public happiness."

Jefferson urged massive immigration to the new United States.

Founder John Adams was in agreement, for reasons of compassion: "It is our business to render our country an asylum, worthy to receive all who may fly to it."

However, aging Founder Ben Franklin still wasn't so sure: "In short unless the stream of their importation could be turned from this to other colonies . . . they will soon so outnumber us, that all the advantages we have will not in my opinion be able to preserve our language, and even our government will become precarious."

⭐ George Washington Disagrees with Himself

George Washington was certainly pro-growth, but even our first president had mixed feelings about immigrants. In 1783 he wrote that America "is open to receive not only the opulent and respectable stranger, but"—striking Adams' note of compassion— "the oppressed and persecuted of all nations

George Washington

and religions; whom we shall welcome to a participation in all of our rights and privileges, if by decency and propriety of conduct they appear to merit the enjoyment." But then, in letters he wrote during 1794: "I have no intention to invite immigrants, even if there are no restrictive acts against it. I am opposed to it altogether."

Rumblings of resentment trickled from the leaders to the general population. Not everyone agreed that immigration was necessarily a good thing. Fears flared that the newcomers were brutes, invaders, scary people who would contaminate the new country.

The cycle of tolerance versus hostility had begun.

An Anti-Immigrant Poem from 1786

"Let Dutchmen come and drain your bogs,
Let Frenchmen come and feast on frogs,
Let Jews among you toil and sweat.
Let stout Hibernians [Irish] children get.

Our Commonwealth is like a custard!
The eggs are citizens if you please,
The rotten ones are refugees.
A single rotten egg shall spoil
The largest custard you can boil."

—"The Custard," from a 1786 newspaper

CHAPTER FOUR

★ ★ ★

Hamilton versus Jefferson

It wasn't long before Americans craved laws that would sort out immigration.

★ THE LAW STEPS IN ★

To make laws we needed a Congress. The very first Congress, in 1790, dealt with the question of citizenship for immigrants who were already here. The 1790 Naturalization Law was the first of our many laws to address the complicated topic. It stated that newcomers ("aliens") who were "free white persons" of good character could apply to be citizens ("naturalized") after living here two years. According to the racist ideas of the times, the law excluded American Indians, indentured servants, enslaved people, and free blacks.

To apply for citizenship, an immigrant could file a Petition for Naturalization. Once convinced of the applicant's good moral character, the court would administer an oath of allegiance to support the Constitution of the United States. But the pendulum of pro- and con-immigration kept swinging. The Act of 1790 was repealed, or struck down, by the Naturalization Act of 1795, which extended the residence requirement to five years.

Then came the Naturalization Act of 1798 (part of the controversial Alien and Sedition Acts), which extended it to fourteen years.

Current events shaped the laws. In 1798 President John Adams wanted to strengthen national security during an undeclared naval war with France. He signed off on the Alien and Sedition Acts, "sedition" referring to resistance to American law. This was a set of bills that made it harder for an immigrant to become a citizen.

Besides the Naturalization Act, it included the Alien Friends Act. Not especially friendly, this gave the government the power to deport, or kick out, noncitizens who were deemed "dangerous to the peace and safety of the United States" at any time. The Alien Enemies Act authorized the president to do the same to any male citizen of a hostile nation above the age of fourteen during times of war.

The overall effect of the Alien and Sedition Acts was

to make it harder for immigrants to become citizens, while at the same time allowing their deportation if they were suspected of disloyalty.

Not everyone approved—Thomas Jefferson, for example, did not, but founder Alexander Hamilton was one who did. He said, "The mass [of immigrants] ought to be obliged to leave the country." But he did urge exceptions, specifically for some foreign merchants and those "whose demeanor among us has been unexceptionable."

Perhaps the Ultimate Immigrant Story— Alexander Hamilton

Alexander Hamilton

Alexander Hamilton was an immigrant from the British West Indies in the Caribbean. As a penniless but obviously bright young orphan of about sixteen, he was sponsored by a group of wealthy local men to pursue his education and reinvent himself in New York City. At the start of the American Revolutionary War in 1775, he joined a militia, eventually ascending to the role of senior aide to General George Washington, the American commander in chief. Hamilton was a key Founder—most notably as architect of the new nation's financial system. He died at age forty-nine in a duel with Aaron Burr. But he lives on by way of *Hamilton*, a Broadway musical that has become part of American culture.

For a new immigrant, Hamilton struck a snobbish tone: "The safety of a republic depends essentially on the energy of a common national sentiment; on a uniformity of principles and habits; on the exemption of the citizens from foreign bias, and prejudice; and on that love of country which will almost invariably be found to be closely connected with birth, education, and family."

Hamilton was an elitist who was more pro-aristocrat that most of the Founders. He didn't trust the "common people" and in fact had contempt for them. Contradicting his own immigrant story, he insisted that "foreigners will generally be apt to bring with them attachments to the persons they have left behind; to the country of their nativity, and to its particular customs and manners."

Thomas Jefferson completely disagreed, and he led the opposition to this harsh new policy. He became the president after John Adams. With his victory in the election of 1800, he brought most of the Alien and Sedition provisions to an end. Three of the acts were repealed. (But the Alien Enemies Act remained in effect.)

Finally (for the time being), the Naturalization Law of 1802 replaced the other laws. Under the 1802 version:

+ the "free white" requirement remained in place;
+ the alien had to declare, at least three years in advance, his intent to become a US citizen;
+ the previous fourteen-year residency requirement was reduced to five years; and
+ resident children of naturalized citizens were to be considered citizens (a key provision that would become important later).

Laws on the topic would continue to seesaw in much the same way throughout our history, reflecting America's dreams and fears as they shifted.

But Thomas Jefferson had cleared the way for immigrants to settle the new country from coast to coast.

Thomas Jefferson

CHAPTER FIVE

★ ★ ★

America Opens
Its Arms

The 1820s ushered in a roaring wave of migration. Over the next sixty years, about fifteen million immigrants, mainly German and Irish, made their way to the United States.

These new settlers had tempting choices for what to do and where to go. Farming was the most popular, with the promise of cheap land beckoning arrivals to the Midwest and Northeast. Big cities—New York, Boston, Philadelphia, and Baltimore—drew others who took on all kinds of jobs.

The settlement of the American Midwest spiked after the opening of the Erie Canal in 1825, which created a water route from the Great Lakes to the rapidly expanding port of New York. Industrial development, particularly in textile production, came to New England.

★ IMMIGRANTS WELCOME! ★

America was open for business, and the need for immigrant labor was high. The Midwest was turning into one of the world's most fertile agricultural regions, and it demanded new people. Several states were so welcoming that they allowed immigrants, including some women, to vote, even if they weren't citizens yet. Groups that might have been enemies back in Europe—Germans, Norwegians, Swedes, Bohemians—lived side by side in peace.

In 1841, President John Tyler struck a friendly note, urging foreigners "to come and settle among us as members of our rapidly growing family."

★ Astonishing Numbers

"In four days 12,000 persons were landed for the first time upon American shores. A population greater than that of some of the largest and most flourishing villages of the state was thus added to the city of New York within 96 hours."

—*the* New York Times, *April 2, 1852*

In 1855 the main entry point for European arrivals became Castle Garden in Manhattan. Once a fort,

it made a useful immigrant processing center. Arrivals had to pay fifty cents (approximately fourteen dollars in today's currency), and just about everyone was allowed in, except "any convict, lunatic, idiot, or any person unable to take care of himself or herself without becoming a public charge."

★ BRIEF HISTORY OF GERMANS IN AMERICA ★

Germantowns sprang up—tight-knit communities of people from Sweden, Norway, Denmark, Bohemia, and various regions of what in 1871 would become Germany. The cities of Cincinnati, Milwaukee, and St. Louis formed a sort of German triangle.

★ Immigrant Story—Levi Strauss

Levi Strauss

At age eighteen, Levi Strauss came to New York City from present-day Germany with his family and became a citizen in 1853. Joining his brothers' successful business selling textiles and clothing, he moved from New York City to San Francisco to open his own branch. He had a brainstorm: the men doing manual labor to build the West needed a new kind of pants. He designed sturdier work pants, made of blue denim, with rivets. Strauss is considered the inventor of blue jeans. With a friend he began to manufacture them, and when he died in 1902, his net worth was estimated in the hundreds of millions.

By 1900, 2.7 million Germans made up the largest total percentage of immigrants in the country. Nearly 20 percent of Americans can trace their ancestors back to Germany.

But prejudice against Germans still lingered long past Ben Franklin's day. Non-Germans feared them because they tended to keep speaking German, educating their children in German, maintaining their own culture, more so than other immigrant groups. At one point there were more than seven hundred German-language newspapers in America.

★ Immigrant Story—Edward Stratemeyer

The son of a German immigrant who came during the Gold Rush of 1849, Edward Stratemeyer adored reading. Put to work in his father's tobacco store at an early age, he started writing a story on a piece of brown wrapping paper. A magazine bought it for six times his weekly pay at the store. Wisely, he turned to writing full-time, becoming one of the most prolific writers ever. In the creation of thousands of books, he hired other writers to help, forming the Stratemeyer Literary Syndicate. He gained millions of readers with his inexpensive series: the Bobbsey Twins, Tom Swift, plus the Hardy Boys and Nancy Drew, which his daughters took over after his death, leaving an indelible mark on American fiction for children.

Ignored by those prejudiced again them was the fact that Germans actually tended to assimilate quickly and begin prospering. Many brought skills from the Old World with them and resumed their careers as bakers, butchers, carpenters, printers, and musicians.

⭐ Immigrant Story—Frederick Trump

To avoid fulfilling his military service in the Imperial German Army, Frederick Trump immigrated to Castle Garden at the age of sixteen, in 1885. He moved in with his older sister and worked as a barber for the next six years. He moved West and

made his fortune by operating restaurants and boarding houses in mining towns. In Seattle he bought the Poodle Dog, which he renamed the Dairy Restaurant, supplying food, alcohol, and "rooms for ladies," which generally indicated prostitution. Continuing to buy real estate, he died a wealthy man at forty-nine in the 1918 flu pandemic. His grandson is Donald Trump, the forty-fifth president of the United States, who, ironically, made anti-immigration his signature issue.

Frederick Trump

The uncertainty of war always drives fear of immigrants to new heights, and during World War I, when America was at war with Germany, prejudice spiked. German Americans were suspected of disloyalty. Many were jailed, attacked by mobs, and even lynched.

Ted Geisel, aka Dr. Seuss

⭐ Immigrant Story—Ted Geisel (Dr. Seuss)

All four of Ted Geisel's grandparents were German immigrants. In his hometown of Springfield, Massachusetts, his family was often treated as outsiders. During World War I, with America fighting Germany, prejudice was out in the open. As a young teen Ted was chased and beaten up. The bullying led to a major theme of compassion and tolerance in his famous books for children.

After World War I, the German community was never as strong, and became less visible. So much prejudice remained that some people, such as those running for office, tended not to publicize their German roots.

★ BRIEF HISTORY OF THE IRISH IN AMERICA ★

Between 1847 and 1852, almost a million Irish moved to America with the most basic motive of all: to eat. Another million people, left behind, were dying of starvation.

The Irish Potato Famine was caused by a previously unknown fungus. It wiped out the potato crop just at a time when too many people depended on a single type of potato for daily meals.

Run as a colony of the vast British Empire, Ireland was considered a food-producing operation, exporting its food elsewhere. After the potato blight, people in Ireland asked the government to close the Irish ports to keep food inside the country. The British refused and at the same time blamed the poor for their own poverty—creating the myth that the Irish were simply lazy, socially backward, and uncivilized.

Irish Catholics desperate to escape the famine and migrate here were primarily unskilled workers. They did the hard labor of building canals and railroads, settling in cities. Many Irish went to the textile mill towns of the Northeast, while others became longshoremen in the growing Atlantic and Gulf port cities. They faced serious discrimination—considered uneducated, inferior, and bearers of germs—with signs on businesses declaring "No Irish Need Apply."

By 1860, Catholics, especially Irish Catholics, made up 12 percent of our population. The surge in numbers felt threatening to the Protestants, who were in the majority.

★ THOSE WHO KNOW NOTHING ★

These newest arrivals spurred America's first organized bout of nativism, the prejudice against newcomers. It topped a resentment of immigrants in general with a particular dread of Catholicism.

Conspiracy theorists seriously believed that Catholics were an overwhelming security threat to the nation. They called it Popery: the Catholic Church was led by the Pope in Rome, and some feared the Pope would take over America, joining forces with Catholics around the world to overthrow the new country. America would no longer be a proud independent nation, some Americans feared, but part of a regime that could tell them what religion to practice.

> "It is a fact, that Popery is opposed in its very nature . . . to our form of government."
> —Samuel Morse, inventor of the telegraph, 1835

In the decades just before the US Civil War (1861–1865), this nativism spawned a powerful movement and even a political party that made anti-immigration and anti-Catholicism its focus. It started out as a secret group called the American Party, or (ironically) the Native American Party. They campaigned to make it *twenty-one years* before an immigrant could become a citizen.

When members were asked about their organization, they were told to reply, "I know nothing." Opponents were quick to label them the Know Nothing party.

Future president Abraham Lincoln, then a forty-six-year-old Illinois state legislator, despised the Know Nothings. In a letter, he claimed they would rewrite the Declaration of Independence to read "all men are created equal, except Negroes and foreigners and Catholics." His opposition to nativism delighted the German voters in Pennsylvania and several other states, and their support was critical to his later presidential victory.

The Irish, meanwhile, worked their way out of poverty. They succeeded at assimilating in all areas, especially in politics, rising to powerful positions in Boston and New York.

★ Immigrant Story—Joseph P. Kennedy, Sr

All four of Joseph's grandparents immigrated to Massachusetts in the 1840s to escape the Irish famine. In Boston, Irish Catholics were strictly excluded by the upper class. But Kennedy fought the prejudice and went to Harvard College, made a fortune as a businessman, and ascended in politics. He encouraged his sons and daughters to play a role in American political life, which they did as the fabled Kennedy dynasty. In 1960, his son John F. Kennedy was elected, against all odds, as the

Joseph Kennedy Sr.

first Irish Catholic president—a huge deal at the time. Kennedys still serve as elected officials at the state and national level today.

★ WHAT THE CIVIL WAR MEANT FOR IMMIGRATION ★

During the Civil War, the government's focus was on keeping the nation together, not immigration. Newcomers continued to arrive, though, with immigrants fighting on both sides of the war, more on the Northern side than the Southern.

When the war ended in 1865, jobs became harder to find, so nativism flared again.

Enslaved African Americans were now freed, and to address their citizenship status, Congress passed the Fourteenth Amendment to our Constitution in 1868.

It granted citizenship to people born within the United States—a group that included enslaved people. It was controversial—Southern states fought against it vigorously, dreading retaliation from former slaves—and it has been interpreted, misinterpreted, and litigated ever since.

But on paper at least, former slaves were now citizens. Southern states immediately began to pass laws denying African Americans the normal rights of citizenship.

Employers were reluctant to hire former slaves, especially in the South, preferring immigrants instead. But once they were here, many employers tended to treat immigrants unfairly, knowing they lacked the power to do anything about it. In response, some workers organized groups called labor unions. They united to fight back against the employers, sometimes violently, to demand better treatment. Nativists called them agitators and found them threatening.

★ Haymarket Riot

Nativists blamed German agitators for the 1886 Haymarket Riot in Chicago. Immigrant workers had gone on strike, refusing to work unless conditions were improved. The strike was peaceful until an unknown person threw a bomb at the police who were trying to break it up. Several workers were killed, and the next day a riot erupted in protest. Seven policemen were killed and sixty injured. The mob action stoked fear and spurred a great anti-immigrant resentment—now the newcomers were called reptiles, rubbish, bad-smelling, and worse. Four of the organizers of the protest were tried and executed.

The Haymarket Riot

In the decades after the Civil War, the technology of ocean travel shifted, and so did the sources of immigration. Previous immigrants had made their way to the United

States on wind-driven ships. Their harrowing journeys took weeks, sometimes months, all the while including dangers like shipwrecks, seasickness, infectious diseases, fires, and storms.

When steamships began to cross the Atlantic in the early 1800s, the trip was still dangerous, but it had become cheaper and had been reduced to only a week to ten days. Steam transportation made it possible for larger ships to bring larger loads of immigrants. This made it easier for people to come from southern and eastern Europe, areas undergoing the same economic transitions that western and northern Europe had earlier experienced. Most of the new immigrants could no longer earn a living in their old countries, and most were young, as with earlier immigrants.

This wave, or more accurately a flood, of immigrants included Italians, Greeks, Hungarians, Poles, as well as several million Jews fleeing violent, government-sponsored persecution in Russia and eastern Europe.

It's hard to believe now, but these newcomers were looked down on because they were not considered white. They were "swarthy," to use Ben Franklin's word. Even the newly assimilated Germans and Irish felt superior.

America was taking another swing toward restricting immigration. Some states started to pass their own immigration laws, which prompted the US Supreme

Court to rule in 1875 that immigration was a federal (national) responsibility, and not up to the states. A national superintendent of immigration was appointed, and by 1890 Congress was marking funds to build the first federal immigrant processing center.

Immigration was about to become considerably more organized and official.

CHAPTER SIX

★ ★ ★

Annie Moore and the Millions Who Followed

Anew era in immigration was ushered in by a fifteen-year-old girl unaccompanied by parents. Standing at the head of a long line, Annie Moore had just shepherded

her two younger brothers all the way from County Cork, Ireland. For being first in the line, perhaps bewildered by all the fuss, Annie was awarded a gold coin and a certificate.

★ ELLIS ISLAND OPENS ★

That day in 1892 was the grand opening of Ellis Island, the immigrant processing center off the coast of Manhattan. Castle Island was no longer big enough to process the thousands of people who were arriving daily. This was the new place for doctors and legal inspectors to check out the arrivals, looking for medical problems or any other reason to turn people away.

We think of Ellis Island as *the* symbol of American immigration, even though it actually came comparatively late in our history.

It was an immediate magnet. Over the years, from 1892 to 1954, Ellis Island processed over twelve million immigrants, sometimes as many as ten thousand people a day. One-fourth of all Americans can trace their ancestry to this island.

★ A Quick History of the Island

The island was at first a home to sea gulls, then to Leni-Lenape Indians. In the 1660s the Dutch West Indian Company bought the islands around Manhattan from the Indians. By the time of the American Revolution, one island was owned by Samuel Ellis, who ran a tavern nearby catering to fishermen. Ellis's heirs sold the island to New York State, which sold it to the federal government. For years it was deserted, mainly used as a place where pirates were hanged. During the War of 1812, landfill was brought in to turn it into a useful fort. Afterward the fort was no longer needed, but a place to process the new immigrants was. Workers used landfillfrom the dirt dug out to make New York's subway tunnelsto increase its size to six acres.

After their grueling journey—especially for the poorest, in the filthy steerage area below deck, with no fresh air and primitive conditions—new arrivals were numb. Exhausted and afraid, most of them didn't speak English.

Annie Moore and the others would have been experiencing a roller coaster of emotions. All were greeted—and perhaps soothed—by the sight of an immense copper woman holding a torch, with a broken chain at her feet, representing the Roman goddess of liberty.

The Statue of Liberty, Another Immigrant Story

The symbol of America—the Statue of Liberty—was a gift from France in honor of America's ideals and friendship with the country. The statue was constructed in France, disassembled and put into crates for its voyage here, then reassembled. Lights inside the torch beckon newcomers. On it is inscribed the date of our Declaration of Independence, as well as "The New Colossus" poem by Emma Lazarus. A dedication ceremony was held in 1886, with an enormous parade of excited Americans. President Grover Cleveland declared that the statue's "stream of light shall pierce the darkness of ignorance and man's

oppression until Liberty enlightens the world." It continues to rise from the skyline of New York, and since 1933 has been maintained as a museum and national park.

At Ellis Island, all immigrants were not created equal. Travelers with money, in first or second class, could be inspected while still on board and were free to bypass the island.

The poor were herded to the island, carrying their possessions in cardboard boxes, baskets, and leather sacks. Sometimes they wore all their clothing, layering up so as not to have more to pack.

Then they passed through the Great Hall, waiting in long lines, hoping to be accepted into America.

Because not everyone was.

★ REASONS AN ARRIVAL COULD GET REJECTED ★

Even as they waited, the newcomers were being watched. Women and girls traveling alone were not allowed to leave until a male relative came to claim them. Inspectors were on the lookout for any reason to reject one of the new arrivals—any physical disability or disease or defect that could affect their ability to earn a living.

Immigrant Story—Isaac Asimov

Isaac Asimov was born to a Jewish family in Russia. His family came to Brooklyn, New York, when he was three years old (and he became a citizen five years later, in 1928). His parents owned various candy stores, in which all family members worked. The stores sold newspapers and magazines, which gave Asimov an endless supply of new reading material he couldn't have afforded otherwise. He became an unusually prolific writer, going on to write or edit more than five hundred books. He was one of the most beloved names in science fiction, especially famous for the Foundation series, the Galactic Empire series, and the Robot series.

When arrivals got to the doctors, they were first checked for infectious diseases, like lice or tuberculosis. Everyone dreaded the test for trachoma—which was then a very contagious eye disease causing blindness—because a small metal hook was used to lift up the eyelid. Doctors checked for people considered "defective"—for those displaying signs of physical disability, such as limping, or breathing with difficulty, as well as those displaying signs of intellectual disability or mental illness.

Doctors used chalk to mark clothes. H was for breathlessness, indicating heart problems, L was for lameness, X was for suspected mental illness.

The inspections mostly took three to five hours—speed was important with so many pouring in. The immigrants might not have realized it at the time, but the odds were greatly in their favor. Estimates vary, but anywhere from .5 percent to 1.5 percent of all Ellis Island immigrants were rejected, perhaps two of every hundred. During World War I, when immigration slowed, allowing for more careful inspection, the percentage of rejections rose to some five out of every hundred.

⭐ Grover Cleveland, Pro-Immigrant

The "stupendous growth [of the United States] is largely due to the assimilation and thrift of millions of sturdy and patriotic adopted citizens . . . now numbered among our best citizens."
—President Grover Cleveland, 1897

Some inspectors were crabby—"I get so sick handling these dirty bums coming over here to this country," said one. But most followed their training to be kind and considerate. Harsh language and rough handling weren't tolerated. The inspectors were frequently immigrants themselves or had immigrant parents.

One doctor would give a pep talk to calm people down. "You are coming to the land of opportunity. You will have a chance to work, to live, and enjoy life. The police will not bother you."

To ease the transition, helpers were on hand —missionaries, private citizens, churches, and aid societies.

★ Changing Names at Ellis Island

The myth persists that when inspectors couldn't pronounce a name foreign to them, they arbitrarily changed it to something simpler—Petrasovich became Preston, for example. In fact, some immigrants did come to America with new names. But it was usually the case that they changed it themselves, before arrival or sometime afterward, wanting to seem more American and blend in. Most inspectors spoke several languages and wouldn't have been flummoxed by unusual names.

Over time, as officials tried to control the flow, more and more reasons for rejection were added. After 1901, when President William McKinley was assassinated by an anarchist, someone opposed to the American government, immigration officers were allowed to ask about political beliefs, trying to keep out anarchists. By 1917 arrivals had to prove they could read. There were restrictions against "idiots, insane persons, paupers," and, later, alcoholics.

★ LIKE A LITTLE CITY ★

Ellis Island had dorms for those kept overnight for observation or treatment, and restaurants with long wooden tables. The food was nutritious if bland, perhaps boiled rice with milk for breakfast, lamb and vegetables for lunch, bologna and mixed salad for dinner. There was a post office and a hospital to hold those detained until they were well. There were banks to exchange money, baths, laundries, too few bathrooms (and no toilet paper), courtrooms, offices for charities and church groups and interpreters—which were available in thirty-seven languages, from Arabic to Yiddish.

★ Melting Pot

The Melting Pot was a 1908 play by British author Israel Zangwill. It included the line "America is God's crucible, the great melting pot where all the races of Europe are melting and re-forming!" Though often disputed, the term took off as the perfect description of America.

★ WHERE NEXT? ★

Many Ellis Island arrivals stayed on in New York. It was right there, teeming with opportunities to work, and relatives were often already living there. The city became a hub thriving with businesspeople speaking dozens of languages, and it would turn into the most diverse city in the United States. By 1869, 69 percent of New Yorkers had been born in another country.

In part because other neighborhoods didn't want them, the new arrivals created isolated islands of people from their homeland. Immigrants tended to stay on their own blocks, looking out for each other. Taken advantage of by greedy landlords and uncaring politicians, they paid high rent and were forced to cram together, ten to fifteen to a room, in rickety apartments called tenements. They had dreadful sewage conditions and lacked adequate light or ventilation, so diseases spread quickly. For new immigrants there was no garbage collection—roving pigs did the job—and there were no social services.

★ Immigrant Story—Annie Moore

Like most families, the Moores didn't cross over together. Annie's parents had come from Ireland three years earlier in search of work and were waiting for her and her brothers. She spent the rest of her life in the same Lower East Side neighborhood. Eventually she married a bakery clerk and had eleven children—with child mortality rates high, only half made it to adulthood. She died at the age of fifty.

The tenements were what we would today call slums—unhealthy, miserable places to live. Those already established here either didn't pay much attention or blamed the immigrants themselves for their living conditions. They must be too lazy to improve their lot, residents grumbled.

★ HOW THE OTHER HALF LIVES ★

Someone who studied the tenements and strongly disagreed with the condemnation was journalist (and an immigrant from Denmark) Jacob Riis. In 1890 he used the new invention of flash photography to expose the dreadful conditions in his landmark book *How the Other Half Lives*. His shocking exposé roused many people's sympathy and led slowly to reform. Theodore Roosevelt, then governor of New York, signed the Tenement House Act of 1901, which led to significant improvements.

President Theodore Roosevelt, Pro-Immigrant

"It is unwise to depart from the old American tradition and to discriminate for or against any man who desires to come here and become a citizen . . . We cannot afford to consider whether he is Catholic or Protestant, Jew or Gentile; whether he is Englishman or Irishman, Frenchman or German, Japanese, Italian, Scandinavian, Slav, or Magyar."

71

—Theodore Roosevelt, 1905

Churches were important to the new arrivals and took the lead in starting up schools and hospitals. In time, there were settlement houses where social workers helped newcomers find jobs, get healthcare, and learn English.

The new people continued the trend of working hard and gravitating toward certain jobs. Italians, for example, were barbers, shoemakers, newsboys, and longshoremen. Germans ran breweries and saloons and were peddlers.

Childcare was not as big a problem as you might think—everyone worked, including children.

Jewish family sewing in a tenement

⭐ Impressions of New York

"I was bewildered at the sight of trains running overhead, under my very feet, trolleys clanging, thousands upon thousands of taxis tearing around corners, and millions of people rushing and pushing through the screaming noise day in and day out. To me this city appeared as a tremendous overstuffed roar, where people just burst with a desire to live."

—Morris Shapiro, Russian immigrant, speaking of his arrival in 1923

This particular wave of immigrants reached tsunami level in 1907, the peak year at Ellis Island. Some 1.4 million immigrants were received, with an all-time daily high on April 17—when the day's total was 11,747. Seventy immigrant stations existed, but 90 percent of immigrants were still entering through Ellis Island, mostly coming from Russia, Italy, and Austria-Hungary.

⭐ Stranger in a Strange Land

For immigration in fiction, there are many great novels, but perhaps one of the most emotional is a picture book. Shaun Tan's The Arrival is a story told in pictures about just how disorienting the immigrant experience can be.

Many who passed through Ellis Island and survived an often difficult life in New York eventually made their way to other cities. They comprised the bulk of the American industrial labor pool. New industries emerged, such as steel, coal, automobile, textile, and garment production, enabling the United States to revolutionize itself as one of the world's economic giants.

★ Immigrant Story—Nikola Tesla

Nikola Tesla sailed from Serbia in 1884, arriving in New York with four cents in his pocket, a few of his own poems, calculations for a flying machine, and plans to be a brilliant inventor. With practical experience in electrical engineering, he was first hired by Thomas Edison, but the two inventors were on different and competing paths. Becoming a citizen at age thirty-five, Tesla eventually obtained around three hundred worldwide patents for his inventions, the most famous being his contributions to the design of the modern alternating current (AC) electricity supply system. A visionary and an eccentric, he was handicapped in his goals by lack of funds. But his legacy

Nikola Tesla

lives on in books, movies, TV, music, live theater, comics, and video games. The fancy electric car called Tesla (promoted by Elon Musk, another immigrant) is named for him.

★ BLOWBACK ★

The arrival of immigrants moving on from New York, of course, was not without blowback. All groups were discriminated against by those who were already here, but the Irish still got the worst of it. "Any country or color—except Irish" read want ads. Catholic churches were attacked and burned.

Immigrant Story—Júlia Warhola

Júlia Warhola came from a peasant family in present-day Slovakia, following her husband to Pittsburgh, Pennsylvania, in 1921. She loved drawing—especially angels and cats—and did many crafts, including decorating Easter eggs in the Ukrainian tradition. She encouraged her three children Paul, John, and Andrew to express themselves artistically. After her husband died, she moved to New York City to take care of Andrew—a successful commercial artist now known as Andy Warhol—and his twenty-five cats. She continued to prefer her peasant clothes over ones he tried to buy for her at Macy's. She worked on several of his early projects and won awards for her decorative lettering. As for Andy, he became one of the most famous pop artists of all time, noted in particular for images of Campbell's soup cans.

The newcomers' numbers, the way they crowded into cities, and the usual human instinct to resent foreigners led to a greater and greater show of nativism, even xenophobia—an extreme fear of another culture. Many Americans—mainly the rich, white, native-born—considered immigrants—mostly poor, "non-white," from unfamiliar places—to pose a serious danger to the nation's health and security.

From 1894 to 1921, a group of businessmen formed the Immigration Restriction League to do all they could to discourage newcomers. In particular, they regarded immigrants from southern and eastern Europe as racially inferior to Anglo-Saxons and a threat to the American way of life.

The immense wave pouring through Ellis Island ended in 1914 with the beginning of World War I. Anti-immigration feeling surged, and immigration slowed.

★ END OF ELLIS ISLAND ★

From the late 1920s onward, Ellis Island was mostly used to *deport* people, not welcome them. During World

War II, with fear of foreigners surging, it housed people thought to threaten the United States—some seven thousand "enemy aliens" from countries we were at war with—German, Italian, and Japanese—people suspected of spying.

Over the three decades after 1954, when it officially closed, it fell into decay. The sea gulls took over Ellis Island once again.

But it was too crucial a part of American history to forget. The National Park Service finally begin restoring it in 1984, opening it as a museum in 1990. In 2015 it was renamed the Ellis Island National Museum of Immigration. Millions of tourists pour into the museum every year to honor their ancestors.

The statue of Annie Moore guards it.

CHAPTER SEVEN

★ ★ ★

Poems on
the Walls

While all of this was occurring on the East Coast, another, less famous, immigrant processing center was in operation over on the West Coast.

The Angel Island Immigration Station was sometimes called the Ellis Island of the West. But differences abounded.

The biggest one was that at Angel Island the majority of the immigrants were not coming from Europe, but from Asian countries such as China, Japan, and India. And the center wasn't meant so much to welcome immigrants to the United States as to keep them out.

To understand this more, we need to look at the strong current of racism against Asians in America.

★ GOLD! ★

Throughout most of the 1800s, as the country expanded westward and workers were needed, America placed no constraints on immigration.

After 1848, the California Gold Rush attracted hundreds of thousands of would-be miners from the eastern states, Latin America, Australia, and Europe. California became a state in 1850 with a population of about ninety thousand.

America presented a great temptation to the vast population in China. China held one-fifth of all people in the world, with many living in desperate poverty. When gold was discovered in California, the chance to earn a fortune was just over the horizon. Chinese began immigrating during the Gold Rush of 1848, eager to dig for gold.

This set off a vicious strain of racism. Mainly, the Chinese were unfamiliar to those already here, considered exotic, with many calling them unsuitable Americans due to their appearance. They had different foods and different religions (one of which was Buddhism, a religion originating in ancient India, which nativists found even more frightening than Catholicism). They were called vampires, scum, and worse. Just as European Americans looked down on American Indians and enslaved blacks, not considering them equal human beings, so too they looked down on the Chinese.

Californians worried that Chinese laborers would take jobs other than mining. Some Californians called for laws to bar them on the basis that they were incapable of assimilation and were a danger to the nation's peace and security.

A "Chinese Must Go" movement arose. Its leader was Denis Kearney (who as it happened was born in Ireland), founder of the Workingmen's Party of California, which formed in reaction to a time of heavy unemployment. Kearney blamed the whole problem on Chinese labor, and he ended every one of his speeches with, "And whatever happens, the Chinese must go!"

★ Frederick Douglass Objected

"I want a home here not only for the Negro. . . . I want the Asiatic to find a home here in the United States, and feel at home here, both for his sake and for ours. Right wrongs no man."
—*African American social reformer Frederick Douglass in a speech, 1869*

Nativists succeeded in barring the Chinese from mining as well as fishing. This left them to find low-wage work most whites didn't want to do, like opening laundries and being migrant farm workers. They were allowed to open restaurants, known as "chow chows," to feed the miners, serving Americanized versions of Chinese food, like chop suey and chow mein.

⭐ Immigrant Story—Wong Chin Foo

Wong Chin Foo was brought here by a missionary in 1876. An educated missionary himself, he soon mastered English and started out as a lecturer, trying to explain Chinese customs to Americans.

He started a newspaper called *Chinese American* (the first time this term was used in print) trying to humanize his people to those who had zero knowledge of China, and he testified in Congress against anti-Chinese laws. He used food to raise awareness—the dumplings, dishes we would now call stir-fries, the wonder of soy sauce. After tempting Americans to try it, he hoped they would go on to develop more empathy. He returned to China in 1898 to reunite with his family. But by 1903 there were around 350 chop suey houses in New York.

But resistance mounted. Whites tried to undercut the Chinese share of the laundry business. Chinese were not allowed to vote, to marry whites, to testify in court, or to become citizens. Chinese children were not allowed to go to public school.

Anti-Chinese racism grew deadly. The Chinese could

be randomly attacked on the streets, with the police offering them no protection. In 1871, a mob broke into a riot in Los Angeles, destroying homes and businesses, looting, and lynching seventeen Chinese immigrants, with little response from the police. In 1885, nearly thirty Chinese immigrants were killed in a riot in Rock Springs, Wyoming. Mob riots broke out all through the 1870s and '80s, with whites feeling free to kill at will.

★ Immigrant Story—Chang and Eng Bunker

The most well-known Asian Americans of the nineteenth century were Chang and Eng. The conjoined Thai brothers were called Siamese twins because Thailand was then known as the Kingdom of Siam. A British sea captain brought them here, making his fortune by exhibiting them in theaters. At twenty-one the brothers began managing themselves and became enormously wealthy. They retired in their late twenties to North Carolina, a state with no Asians, in 1839. The two took up farming and married two white sisters. They applied for and received US citizenship (adopting the last name Bunker). With their celebrity status, the twins faced surprisingly little prejudice. They did tours of San Francisco in 1860 with no problem, even though the tide against Asians was beginning to turn.

Chinese railroad workers laying track

Meanwhile, Congress had approved an ambitious plan to unite the country with railroads, making it easier to travel. The planned new cross-country railroad presented opportunity to thousands of Chinese who were still here after being banned from mining. Starting in 1863, the Chinese provided 80 percent of the back-breaking labor to build the railroads connecting one coast to another.

When the railroad was completed in the early 1900s, the Chinese, no longer welcome as laborers, began moving east.

For their safety, the Chinese formed their own neighborhoods—Chinatowns. These were self-contained, self-sufficient communities, usually in rundown, outlying areas of a city, like cities within cities. Chinatowns sprang up in San Francisco, Los Angeles, and elsewhere.

The Chinese were considered such a novelty in New York City that P. T. Barnum put one person on display in his carnival in 1880, charging admission to see a person from faraway China. Later, a huge Chinatown emerged in Manhattan, inhabited by the largest Chinese population outside of China.

★ A FIRST IN AMERICAN HISTORY ★

Eventually, the "Chinese Must Go" movement helped to get laws passed that all but blocked Chinese people from entering the country.

The 1876 presidential race between Rutherford Hayes and Samuel Tilden influenced this new development. Leading up to the election, the race was so close that it brought California's ongoing fight to push out Chinese immigrants to the national stage.

One senator expressed the prevailing racism: "You cannot work a man who must have beef and bread, and would prefer beer, alongside of a man who can live on rice. It cannot be done."

★ Even the Food

Champions of the Chinese Exclusion Act often cited the weakening effect of Chinese food on the American worker. Labor leader Samuel Gompers wrote a pamphlet titled "Some Reasons for Chinese Exclusion: Meat versus Rice, American Manhood against Asiatic Coolieism: Which shall survive?"

In 1879 California succeeded in barring Chinese immigration, with Congress following suit years three later. The Chinese Exclusion Act of 1882 barred laborers, allowing entrance only to merchants, clergy, diplomats, teachers, and students. Working-class Chinese men and women were only allowed if they could prove that they were related to American citizens.

★ Racist Image

In a popular cartoon from 1881, called "A Statue for Our Harbor," a Chinese man stands on a pedestal surrounded by a harbor in imitation of the Statue of Liberty. His clothes are tattered; his hair is in a long, thin tail; his eyes squint. The words *diseases, filth, immorality,* and *ruin to white labor* float around his head. The image reflects the anti-Chinese sentiment of the time and was used to drum up support for the passage of the Chinese Exclusion Act.

For the first time in American history, people were barred from immigrating because of their race. The United States stopped being a country that welcomed foreigners without restrictions, borders, or gates. Instead, it became a gatekeeping nation.

The first patrols installed along the Mexican border in the 1890s were not to keep out Mexicans, but Chinese trying to enter from the south.

⭐ President Grover Cleveland, Anti-Immigrant

"The experiment of blending the social habits and mutual race idiosyncrasies of the Chinese laboring classes with those of the great body of the people of the United States has been proved . . . to be in every sense unwise, impolitic, and injurious to both nations."

—*President Grover Cleveland, 1888*

In 1889 the Supreme Court upheld the law, ruling the Chinese Exclusion Act constitutional. Chinese Exclusion was going to last for sixty years, from 1882 to 1943, with little protest against it.

⭐ The Supreme Court: Not Always on the Right Side of History

"They remained strangers in the land, residing apart by themselves, and adhering to the customs and usages of their own country. It seemed impossible for them to assimilate with our people, or to make any change in their habits or modes of living. As they grew in numbers each year the people of the coast saw, or believed they saw, in the facility of immigration, and in the crowded millions of China, where population presses upon the means of subsistence, great danger that at no distant day that portion of our country would be overrun by them, unless prompt action was taken to restrict their immigration."

—*Supreme Court ruling, 1889*

★ THE PURPOSE OF ANGEL ISLAND ★

Racist propaganda against the Chinese led to the Chinese Exclusion Act, and then to the federal government creating a special immigration station to monitor the flow of Chinese immigrants.

Located just across from the military prison on Alcatraz Island in San Francisco Bay, Angel Island started operating in 1910. It mainly processed the cases of Chinese laborers, the first group of people to be specifically blocked by federal immigration policy.

Immigrants arrived there from eighty-four different countries—including Japan, India, Russia, and the

CaptionTK?

Philippines, with Chinese immigrants accounting for the largest group. The first Jewish refugees fleeing Nazi Germany would escape to Shanghai, one of the few places that would admit them, then wait for months or years to enter the United States through Angel Island.

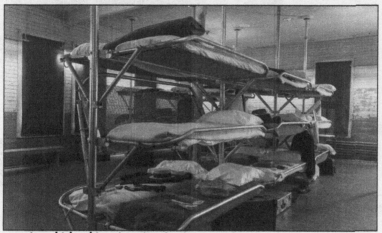

Angel Island Immigration Station

★ Early History of Angel Island

Coastal Miwok Indians were the first inhabitants, using the island as a site for fishing and hunting. Then a Spanish explorer reconstructed it as a cattle ranch. During the Civil War, it was a US Army post. The island caught the attention of immigration officials looking for a detention facility. It seemed ideal because of its isolated location, which made it easy to control newcomers, contain outbreaks of disease, and enforce the new immigration laws.

89

Families being examined at Angel Island

Chinese who sought entry into the United States could be detained for days, weeks, months, even a year or more, as they tried to prove their right to enter. They lived behind fences and barred windows, facing extreme interrogation mostly aimed at detecting fake identity claims.

★ SONS OF PAPER ★

Since the goal of Angel Island was to deport as many Chinese immigrants as possible, the whole process was much more intrusive and demanding for the Chinese compared to other applicants. Applicants had to be on their toes to pass the drill, and some devised ways around it.

Some, mostly males, claimed to be sons of Chinese individuals who were American citizens. Since children of citizens are automatically considered US citizens, they could be admitted. The concept of "paper sons," or, less commonly, "paper daughters," of earlier Chinese immigrants was born—children on paper, but without actual familial ties.

The individual would be bombarded with specific questions that only real family members would be able to answer—details of family history, location of their village, their homes: How many steps led up to your front door? Who lived in the fourth house in the second row of houses in your village?

Applicants would have to commit detailed biographical information to memory in order to pass the tests. If there was any indication that the applicant was lying, the questioning process was prolonged, and if doubts continued, the applicant would be in danger of deportation.

★ Irony

During this time, other Asian countries barred certain immigrants. Japan, for example, banned Chinese and Korean immigration.

Those who successfully made it through would produce elaborate instruction manuals to coach the ones who followed them. Anyone caught with these manuals would most likely be deported.

Those who failed the tests dreaded the shame of returning to China, and sometimes would commit suicide before leaving, or on the ships back to their homeland.

★ "AMERICA HAS POWER, BUT NOT JUSTICE" ★

For some, Angel Island was basically a prison where they could be detained indefinitely.

In the barracks, on the wooden walls and posts, detainees began to write poems expressing their frustration, despair, hopes, and homesickness. They wrote eloquently, using the forms of classical Chinese poetry.

★ Poems in Translation

America has power, but not justice.
In prison, we were victimized as if we were guilty.
Given no opportunity to explain, it was really
    brutal.

With a hundred kinds of oppressive laws, they
    mistreat us Chinese.
It is still not enough after being interrogated and
    investigated several times;
We also have to have our chests examined while
    naked.

Been seven weeks since my imprisonment
On this Island—still I do not know when I can land.
Due to the twists and turns of fate,
Have to endure bitterness and sorrow.

Angel Island, Angel Island, all the people said.
So I thought it would be like heaven.
Yet when the iron gate locks with a clang—
It feels like hell.

At Ellis Island, some 20 percent of arrivals from various countries were detained for further inspection, with only some 2 percent being deported. At Angel Island, 60 percent were detained and 14 percent were deported, mostly Chinese.

Angel Island was finally closed in 1940. Estimates vary, but as many as a million immigrants were processed here.

★ APOLOGIES ★

President Franklin D. Roosevelt was sympathetic to the struggling new immigrants but provided no leadership in this area.

FDR

"Remember always, that all of us, and you and I especially, are descended from immigrants and revolutionists."
—*President Franklin D. Roosevelt, 1938*

But Congress did finally repeal the Chinese Exclusion Act in 1943. During World War II, China had become our ally in fighting Japan. Americans began treating the Chinese with more respect, and the exclusion became a national embarrassment.

FDR

"Nations, like individuals, make mistakes. We must be big enough to acknowledge our mistakes of the past and correct them."
—*President Franklin D. Roosevelt, 1943*

By 1979 Vice President Walter Mondale was declaring that the United States had "failed the test of civilization."

Finally, in 2012, the House of Representatives issued a formal apology for the Chinese Exclusion Act. California representative Judy Chu (the first Chinese American woman elected to Congress) said, "We must finally and formally acknowledge these ugly laws that were incompatible with America's founding principles. By doing so, we will acknowledge that discrimination has no place in our society."

⭐ Immigrant Story—Judy Chu

Judy Chu's parents married in 1948 in Guangdong, a province in southern China, then moved to Los Angeles, and later San Francisco. After earning several degrees and teaching psychology for twenty years, Chu signed up for a brand-new Asian American studies course. "It was like a light went off in my head," she said. She learned about the discrimination Asian immigrants endured and their contributions to American life. "It was the very first time it occurred to me that

Judy Chu

an Asian American woman could be a leader," said Chu, who began volunteering with various causes. She entered politics as a board member for a school district, rising to become the first Chinese American woman elected to the US Congress, as a representative for the district that includes Pasadena and the west San Gabriel Valley of southern California. She serves on many committees and has helped immigrants as one of her main issues.

★ Irony

Today people of Chinese origin are often called a "model minority"—a group whose members achieve a higher degree of educational and economic success than average. The term, coined in 1966 to describe Asian Americans, is a stereotype—not fair to individuals, putting on too much pressure. It comes from a limited, white point of view, measuring people by how fast they learn English and assimilate into American culture.

Still, damage was done—to the Chinese and to the country. The Chinese Exclusion era put into place the principles that give the federal government vast powers in immigration matters, principles that underwrite our entire system and can be used to justify discrimination.

During World War II, Angel Island served as a prisoner-of-war processing center for the US military. After the war, the island was abandoned and fell into ruin.

★ Immigrant Story—Yo-Yo Ma

Yo-Yo Ma was born to Chinese parents living in France. He was a baby musical genius, trying several instruments before choosing cello at age four. In 1962, when Ma was seven, the family wanted to move to America to join Ma's uncle and to nurture the boy's extraordinary talent. Isaac Stern, a famous violinist (and another immigrant, from Ukraine) provided much-needed support during the immigration process and helped the family get established in New York City. Ma went on to a brilliant career as the most versatile and best-known cellist in the world. Most recently, in

Cellist Yo-Yo- Ma

founding Silkroad, he fosters diversity, in a thrilling musical collaboration among seventeen countries including Mongolia, Syria, Azerbaijan, and Iran—all locations along the historic Eurasian trade route, the Silk Road.

Thanks to pressure from the Chinese American community, it was designated as a state landmark in 1964. The barracks were set for demolition until someone discovered the poetic verses the detainees had carved on the walls. More than two hundred poems have been recovered and restored.

Today Angel Island is a museum commemorating the immigrants and preserving some of the wall poems, now considered precious historical artifacts.

CHAPTER EIGHT

★ ★ ★

More Ebbs and Flows into the 1900s— and Why

Those who looked different, practiced a different religion, or ate different foods continued to face barriers to acceptance in American society.

★ Many Hate Groups in America

America's largest hate group, or organization that advocates hatred on the basis of race or ethnicity, is the Ku Klux Klan. It is a white-supremacist organization, insistent that whites are superior to others. Originally intent on violence against newly freed blacks, it was also anti-Catholic, anti-Semitic, all-around anti-immigrant. In reaction to new laws

Ku Klux Klan parade, 1926

trying to help blacks gain their rights as citizens, the group flourished throughout the 1920s as a major political force. It still has several thousand members today operating in about 130 groups.

★ IMMIGRANTS FROM SOUTH AND EAST INDIA ★

Like the Chinese, Indian immigrants often faced violent opposition.

In 1907, in Bellingham, Washington, an anti-immigrant riot broke out. A hate group called the Asiatic Exclusion League was angry about Indian immigrants getting so many jobs at local lumber mills, where they were considered ideal employees, working hard for low pay. A mob of four hundred to five hundred white men, mostly members of the League, attacked the homes of the Indians. The Indians were mostly Sikhs from the Punjab region of northwest India, but were labeled as Hindus from South Asia by newspapers of the day—"hordes of Hindus" to be feared. The mob threw workers into the streets, beat them up, and destroyed their property.

The police cooperated with the mob by corralling some four hundred beaten Indian immigrants into the basement of city hall, saying it was for their safety. No one was killed, but six Indians were hospitalized, and by the next day over a hundred had been driven out of town. No participants in the mob violence were ever prosecuted.

Similar vicious attacks took place in other Washington and California cities.

★ How Opinions Change in a Hundred Years

"The Hindu is not a good citizen. It would require centuries to assimilate him, and this country need not take the trouble. Our racial burdens are already heavy enough to bear."
—Bellingham Herald, 1907

"It's time to apologize for the venomous racism, for the demeaning talk, for the refusal to defend human beings against the mob because of their skin tone and ethnicity. We apologize to the East Indian people in our community today, and to

any right-thinking person who is disgusted by the actions this newspaper took in one of the darkest times in our community's history. We are disgusted too."
—Bellingham Herald, *2007*

In recognition of the hundredth anniversary of the riots, the mayor of Bellingham proclaimed September 4, 2007, a Day of Healing and Reconciliation, acknowledging and atoning for the violence.

★ MUSLIMS IN AMERICA ★

For most of our history, Muslims were not allowed to become citizens because of the Naturalization Act of 1790, which restricted citizenship to "whites."

But Muslims have been immigrating here since 1869, settling in large numbers in the late nineteenth and early twentieth centuries. First they came from Yemen, Syria, Jordan, Libya, and Palestine, later fleeing persecution from countries all over the world.

They traveled the East Coast, working in grocery stores before setting off west across the prairie as migrant peddlers. They sold needles, thread, and lace when they were poor, linens and prints when they'd had some success. Local American Indians were some of their best customers.

The oldest Muslim congregation in the United States was established in Iowa in 1885. Today there are twenty-five mosques in Iowa, serving the roughly eighty thousand Muslims in the state. Currently, some are under attack from those who fear a Muslim invasion of the country.

⭐ Immigrant Story—Zarif Khan, Hot Tamale Louie

Zarif Khan immigrated in 1909 at around age twelve from an area between Afghanistan and Pakistan. In his early twenties he moved to remote Wyoming, which so desperately needed people that he got a great deal on a parcel of land. Working eighty hours a week, he established himself as an extremely popular Mexican food vendor called Hot Tamale Louie. A local legend, he was part of a whole network of Afghan tamale venders working during this time in every city in the west. Khan applied for citizenship and became the patron of the Muslim community in Wyoming. A year later a court took his citizenship away because he wasn't white, instead a "member of the yellow race." He applied a second time and finally in 1954, after almost fifty years of working here, was made a citizen.

By 1914 Muslims from sixty countries—including present-day Turkey, Morocco, Egypt, Yemen, Syria, and others—had moved here. Many lived in New York City's Little Syria and in Boston. In the 1920s and 1930s, many of these immigrants set out West. A large number of them settled in Detroit, as well as many other Midwestern areas where they worked as farmers. They were met with little resistance except when they tried to become citizens.

Finally, in 1944, a man from Saudi Arabia became a citizen in a court ruling that Arabs be considered part of the white race.

★ Immigrant Story—Luther George Simjian

Luther George Simjian was an Armenian from modern day Turkey who got separated from his family during the Armenian genocide. He was able to escape and come to America in 1920. He lived with relatives in Connecticut, then moved to New York City, where he went on to invent all sorts of creative things, including (in 1959) the first ATM (automated teller machine). He kept inventing until he died at ninety-two.

★ Immigrant Story—Steve Jobs

Apple Inc., the world's largest information technology company, was started by a child of immigrants. Steve Jobs's birth father was Abdulfattah Jandali, a Syrian Muslim immigrant, while his adoptive mother was the daughter of Armenian immigrants. As he was growing up in the Bay Area, his adoptive father built a workbench in the garage that Jobs could use for tinkering. At ten, he was already involved with electronics and asking advice from engineers who lived in his neighborhood. In his early twenties he founded Apple to sell the personal computer

he'd developed. The company was worth over $100 million by the time he was twenty-five. In 2007 Jobs was named the most powerful person in business by Fortune magazine.

Steve Jobs

★ WARS INTERVENE ★

By World War I, immigrants were literally fighting for America and its ideals. A full 18 percent of the American army was born in another country.

When World War I began (1914), hundreds of women found themselves affected by a law that Congress had passed in 1907. The Expatriation Act decreed, among other things, that US women who married noncitizens were no longer Americans. If their husbands later became naturalized citizens, they could go through the naturalization process to regain citizenship. In 1915 the Supreme Court upheld the sexist law, arguing that the women chose to marry knowing this was a consequence, so it wasn't as if they were being forced into it.

Once the war started and we were fighting Germany, American-born women who had married German immigrants who were not yet citizens lost their citizenship. The women had to register as "enemy aliens"—subject to being detained or deported—a hurtful label for women born in America.

Changing the unfair law became an important part of the agenda for the women's suffrage movement. Once American women finally won the right to vote in 1920, they started lobbying Congress, pushing them to recognize that their citizenship should not be tied to that of a husband. They got the law repealed two years later.

Suffragette march

⭐ Immigrant Story—Peg O'Connor

In 1916, before World War I intervened and boats were no longer allowed to leave Ireland, the last boat out carried Peg O'Connor, at age twenty-one.

The Germans had been bombing passenger boats, and Peg had to sign a waiver that she was sailing at her own risk through waters full of enemy submarines. But Peg could see no future for herself back in County Kerry, Ireland. Her cruel father had pulled her out of sixth grade to put her to work on the family farm after her mother died. When her father fell ill, her siblings expected her to

photo TK?

Peg O'Connor

take care of him, but she had had enough of hard
work and poverty. Her journey was rough, but
she made it to Ellis Island, and then to Chicago.
Facing anti-Irish discrimination, she waited tables
and cleaned houses. By marrying Michael Folliard,
a dashing Irish American street car conductor,
Peg automatically became a citizen too, under the
law at that time. They had five children and eight
grandchildren, one of whom is the author of this
book.

During World War I, European governments introduced border passport requirements for security reasons,
as proof of official identity, and to control the number of
people with useful skills who wanted to leave. These con-
trols remained in place after the war, becoming standard,
though controversial. Then, a 1920 international confer-
ence issued guidelines for all passports, guidelines, which
have been refined in the years since then.

★ EMERGENCY QUOTA ACT OF 1921 ★

The world was in upheaval—what with the immense
destruction of the war, plus the Russian Revolution of
1917, as well as the breakup of empires in Europe and
the Middle East. The worldwide stress was causing even
more people to want to flee to America—just at a time
when unemployment was high.

⭐ Immigrant Story—Bela Lugosi

Bela Lugosi had to leave his native Hungary after the failed Hungarian Communist Revolution of 1919. He entered America illegally through New

Orleans as a seaman on a merchant ship and became a citizen in 1931. He was already a stage actor, and in America, along with fellow Hungarian actors, he formed a small touring company, playing for immigrant audiences. He went on to Hollywood, achieving lasting fame for portraying Count Dracula in the 1931 movie *Dracula* and his roles in

Bela Lugosi

other popular horror films. Lugosi is credited with establishing the modern vampire image, complete with Hungarian accent.

So a significant bout of nativism led to a law that proved a turning point in immigration history. In 1921, President Warren Harding signed the Emergency Quota Act, the first law to set numerical quotas controlling who could and couldn't enter.

It used complicated math to establish a National Origins Formula. The formula restricted the number coming in from any one country. The ultimate effect was to give preference to white immigrants from central, northern, and western Europe, severely limiting the numbers from Russia, Italy, eastern and southern Europe, Africa, and the Middle East, and deeming all potential immigrants from Asia unworthy of entry.

Immigration fell sharply in the years after 1921.

1921 anti-immigrant cartoon—"The Only Way to Handle It"

The quota system was not eliminated until President Lyndon B. Johnson's administration in 1965, but in the meantime millions of people, unable to immigrate here, were devastated by it.

★ Anti-Immigrant Testimony

"Physically, the bodies of recent immigrants are sounder than those of the average American stock. But . . . we have recently admitted inferior mental and social qualities of a constitutional nature which neither education nor better environment can be expected to raise above, or even to approximate, the average of the American descended from older immigrants."

—*"Expert" testifying to the House Committee on Immigration and Naturalization, 1922*

"Our capacity to maintain our cherished institutions stands diluted by a stream of alien blood . . . The myth of the melting pot has been discredited . . . The United States is our land . . . We intended to maintain it so. The day of unalloyed welcome to all peoples, the day of indiscriminate acceptance of all races, has definitely ended."

—*Congressman Albert Johnson from Washington State, 1927, spearheading the fight for quotas*

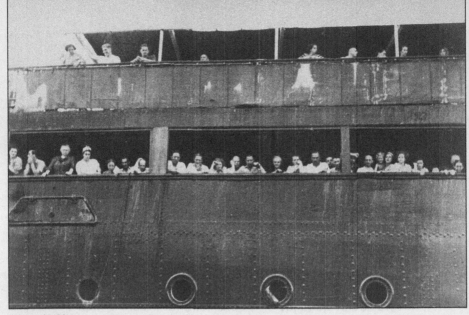

St. Louis, Havana

One of the most tragic effects of the quota system was to prevent entry to large numbers of Jews seeking refuge from Nazis intent on genocide. In 1939, for example, America denied entry to a German ocean liner named the *St. Louis*. It was carrying 930 Jewish refugees from Germany. The ship was forced to return to Europe, where approximately one-fourth of the passengers later died in the Holocaust.

★ Immigrant Story—Ralph Baer

Ralph Baer was born in 1922 in Germany to Jewish parents. When he was a teen, his family was able to flee to New York City from Nazi Germany before the outbreak of World War II.

He took up the study of electronics and proved to be a whiz at it. In 1951 he came up with the idea of playing games on TV screens. He is credited as being the inventor of video games. In 2006 he was awarded the National Medal of Technology for his "pioneering creation . . . of interactive video games." He kept inventing other cool things—from popular video games and electronic greeting cards to a submarine tracking system—until his death at ninety-two.

Ralph Baer

At one point, all the back-and-forth arguments over who could come to America became meaningless. In 1929, the New York stock market crashed, and the resulting Great Depression slammed America hard throughout the 1930s. One out of four Americans had no job.

Immigration dropped to fifty thousand a year—because of the dire conditions here, more people were emigrating, or leaving the country, than immigrating. But the Depression soon spread around the world, with devastating effects.

After the Depression came the cataclysm of World War II, drawing in almost every country in the world.

Among its endless other effects on world history, World War II stopped American immigration altogether for the moment.

CHAPTER NINE

★ ★ ★

A Dark Chapter

The shocking event that brought the United States into World War II was the Japanese bombing of Pearl Harbor in Hawaii on December 7, 1941. More than 2,400 Americans, mostly servicemen, were killed—sending the nation into a tailspin.

Even before the war, the Japanese hadn't been having an easy time of it here.

★ JAPANESE IN AMERICA ★

Shortly after the Chinese immigration wave began, Japanese people followed, escaping poverty in their homeland. By the late 1880s, the number of Japanese immigrants equaled the number of Chinese immigrants, and by 1915 they outnumbered the Chinese.

Japanese immigrants faced the same treatment as Chinese immigrants: they were discriminated against and barred from citizenship. Many were Buddhist, a religion that, because it was so unfamiliar, somehow inspired more terror than Catholicism. They faced organized political opposition from a combination of labor and white supremacist groups.

But they continued to arrive, in search of work. Despite the discouragement, many became successful farmers, which drew great resentment from white farmers. Even children faced discrimination, with San Francisco ordering all Japanese students into segregated "Oriental" schools.

One group, the Asiatic Exclusion League, aimed to stop Japanese immigration completely and created discriminatory laws. "There is no way by which California could be surely Orientalized as by a general influx of Japanese into the ownership or leasing of farms. Also, there is no one who would suffer so immediately under that Orientalization as the white farmer," stated the league in 1913.

Immigration from Japan was curbed in 1907 and fully stopped in 1924.

Known as Issei—meaning first generation—all those who were already here were Japanese citizens, considered non-white, not allowed to become Americans. The second generation, their children, were known as Nisei and were automatically citizens because they were born here. Most Nisei actively embraced America, thought of themselves as proud Americans, spoke English, and preferred American food and customs.

★ Hawaii, Part 1

By 1920, Asians made up 62 percent of the American territory of Hawaii. The 1924 halt of Japanese immigrants didn't apply to Hawaii, which wasn't a state yet and needed workers for its sugar plantations. Anti-Asian racism was a factor in preventing Hawaii from becoming a state for years, until 1959.

★ THE ROUNDUPS BEGIN ★

Nativists were increasingly resentful of Japanese Americans, and then alarmed. After the bombing of Pearl Harbor, within forty-eight hours, they unleashed their anger.

With war raising national hysteria to an unprecedented level, America started doing something unprecedented—imprisoning immigrants.

Remember the Alien Enemies Act from 1798? Now it was used by President Franklin D. Roosevelt to issue

Executive Order 9066. This authorized the military to remove potential enemies from West-Coast states, relocate them in internment camps, and detain them indefinitely. The guiding force behind the order was Earl Warren, then attorney general of California. The purpose of the order was to protect the West Coast from further attack and invasion from "enemy aliens."

FDR's action gave John DeWitt, the Army general in command of the coast, the power to issue orders emptying parts of California, Oregon, Washington, and Arizona. It applied to both Issei—immigrants from Japan, who were precluded from US citizenship by law—and Nisei, their children, who were US citizens by birth.

In writing about "alien enemies," in particular Japanese Americans, DeWitt had said: "The Japanese race is an enemy race and while many second and third generation Japanese born on United States soil, possessed of United States citizenship have become 'Americanized,' the racial strains are undiluted."

DeWitt attempted to justify the military necessity of the roundups with an ironic piece of circular logic: "The very fact that no sabotage has taken place to date is a disturbing and confirming indication that such action will be taken."

After the shock of Pearl Harbor, fear had risen to

such a high level that hardly anyone spoke up to defend the Japanese Americans.

⭐ Hawaii, Part 2

The one place the executive order didn't affect was Hawaii—which was the only place the Japanese had actually attacked. Japanese Americans made up most of the islands' workforce—too valuable to the economy to intern, with not enough police to monitor them.

The roundups began quietly one morning. Some 120,000 people were forced at gunpoint to leave their houses, shops, farms, and fishing boats. Children had to leave school to be united with their families. They were

Japanese child in an internment camp

only allowed to take what they could carry. Anything they left behind had to be sold for next to nothing.

The brutal treatment resembled that of horses or cows. "When they were talking about 'rounding them up,' that's exactly the term that was used for us, in putting us into the camps," said one internee later.

Few spoke up to protest the injustice. Japanese Americans had become so mistrusted that they were widely regarded as spies. Aided by lies in the press, untrue rumors had been spreading: the Japanese were selling fish mixed with ground glass, poisoning the vegetables they sold in the market, hiding shortwave radios in their garden hoses. Supposedly they were planting their crops in arrow formations to direct planes to possible targets, and fishermen had Japanese naval uniforms hidden in their boats, to use for the coming invasion. People believed the Nisei and Issei were automatically disloyal and would aid the invaders.

★ THE CAMPS ★

Internees of all ages were first taken by buses, trains, and trucks to racetracks and fairgrounds used as processing centers. They stayed in animal stables and stalls where livestock had been recently kept. The stench of manure was fresh, and they were literally forced to live like animals.

Japanese family
waiting for evacuation

Then they were shipped to one of ten "relocation centers," primitive camps built in the remote landscapes of the interior West and Arkansas. The locations were on American Indian reservations, among the least pleasant places in the country. Topaz War Relocation Center, for example, was in the Utah desert, where temperatures averaged about 125 degrees.

Years later, internees would recollect the cold, the heat, the wind, the dust—and the isolation.

"Eye-burning dust, and the temperature seemed to stand at 120 degrees for three solid months"—this

121

was how Japanese American sculptor Isamu Noguchi described his time at Poston, situated in the Sonoran Desert of Arizona.

⭐ Immigrant Story—Madeleine Sugimoto

"I think you have to be careful," warned a friend of Madeleine Sugimoto's father after the bombing of Pearl Harbor. She was six years old when her family was sent to an assembly hall near their home in central California. Madeleine thought she was there for a picnic—people from her community were sitting at wooden picnic tables with benches, having a meal. She got tired and asked when they could go home, only to be told they couldn't: they were being shipped to an internment camp in Arkansas. Her father, a well-known artist, was able to put his paintings into storage. Their camp was surrounded by barbed wire, and they lived in army-style barracks covered in tar paper. With her family facing an uncertain future, Madeleine made the best of the camp, finding playmates, joining the Girl Scout troop in the camp, and going to the camp school, where both her parents taught. Later, camp survivors were given twenty-five dollars to start a new life. Madeleine's family went to New York and started over, but they weren't always welcomed. "Some people didn't want to see the Japanese return again," she said. When her father

went to reclaim his paintings, he found that they
had been auctioned off while he was interned.
Madeleine grew up to become a nurse and a
teacher of nursing.

Families could stay together, but living quarters were
shared with strangers with little to no privacy. Some
couldn't even dress themselves privately. There were no
bathrooms in the barracks, so everyone had to line up
outside to use the communal outhouses. Showers were
also taken in open areas. Because of the proximity to so
many people, sickness was prevalent, and numerous people died from the lack of proper medical treatment.

The regime was prisonlike: armed guards, barbed
wire, roll call. Guards with machine guns watched internees from towers, using roving searchlights throughout
the night. Anyone who attempted to escape or failed to
obey orders could be killed. Guards faced little punish-
ment for killing without cause.

Nisei Soldiers

By 1943 the Army was enlisting Nisei soldiers
to fight in Africa and Europe, using them as a
propaganda tool to counter Japanese claims of
American racism. Nisei could escape the camps
if they enlisted, and many jumped at the chance

to prove their loyalty. After the war, President Harry Truman told the all-Nisei 442nd Regimental Combat Team—the most decorated unit in the war, which fought in France, Italy, and North Africa, and suffered heavy casualties: "You fought not only the enemy, but you fought prejudice—and you have won." Their service helped to turn the tide of public opinion against the internment camps.

442nd Regimental Combat team

These weren't concentration camps, like what Nazis were building for people they hated. They weren't exactly jails. What they were is hard to say—"internment camp" doesn't quite convey the outrageousness. The action violated all kinds of rights in our founding documents, like being assumed innocent until proven guilty and being imprisoned without due process of law.

The Supreme Court, which might have protected the Japanese on the basis of how many of their civil rights were being violated, upheld the constitutionality of FDR's order.

★ The ACLU

One of the only groups to protest the internment—unsuccessfully—was the American Civil Liberties Union. It had been formed in 1920 by a group of pacifists and activists (including social worker Jane Addams, author Helen Keller, lawyer Crystal Eastman, and lawyer and later Supreme Court Justice Felix Frankfurter) in an alarmed response to intolerance of free speech. The ACLU's purpose is to defend and preserve rights guaranteed by the Constitution, including those of immigrants. It had little success at first taking civil liberties cases to court, but later won major cases in the Supreme Court that affect the lives of all Americans. Local chapters are active in almost every state, and membership is in the millions.

★ LIFE AT MANZANAR ★

Of the ten internment camps, California's Manzanar was the most notorious. From 1942 to 1945, it held over eleven thousand internees.

People stood in long lines for little food, eating off tin pie plates in big mess halls. They were fed government foods and castoff meat from Army surplus—hot dogs, ketchup, kidneys, Spam, and potatoes. The Japanese diet was ignored.

In the chaos of the dining hall, families weren't allowed to sit together and eat. Teenagers wanted to be with other teenagers. Old people, who had once sat at the extended family table, were isolated. Grandparents, parents, and children broke apart in the face of mess hall dining. Mothers could no longer cook for their children. The family table, with its traditions and conversations, began to fade.

They slept on cots, atop mattresses of straw. There was no privacy in the bathrooms.

Children went to school, though they didn't have textbooks, writing materials, desks, or in most cases, qualified teachers willing to work there. They learned to type on imaginary typewriters and studied chemistry by pretending to mix chemicals they didn't actually have.

★ Immigrant Story—George Takei

George Takei, an actor most famous for his role on *Star Trek*, was born in 1937 to Japanese American parents living in Los Angeles. Between the ages of five and nine, he was interned in an Arkansas camp: "I grew up behind US barbed wire fences." As he recited the Pledge of Allegiance each morning, he "could see from the window the barbed wire and the sentry towers where guards kept guns trained on us." His parents' "only crime was refusing, out of principle, to sign a loyalty pledge" that the American government was requiring of them. "The

George Takei, in Star Trek

authorities had already taken my parents' home on Garnet Street in Los Angeles, their once thriving dry cleaning business, and finally their liberty." Besides acting—including telling his internment story in a Broadway play—he cofounded the Japanese American National Museum.

★ AFTERMATH ★

Not a single instance of spying or attempted invasion was ever prosecuted or proved among the 120,000 internees.

The issue of injustice done to Japanese Americans worked its way through the courts. Finally the Supreme Court ruled that the government could not detain citizens who were loyal to the United States. In December 1944, as the war was ending and America and its allies were winning, Roosevelt rescinded the executive order. Japanese Americans were given train tickets and were able to start leaving the camps.

The last camp was closed in 1946.

⭐ Immigrant Story—Yoshiko Uchida

The night that Pearl Harbor was bombed, Yoshiko Uchida's father, deemed an "enemy alien," was taken away by government officials and sent to an Army camp in Montana. Within months, the rest of Yoshiko's family was given ten days to pack up, allowed to take only what they could carry—which didn't include their collie, Laddie. At age twenty, Uchida was dismayed to leave her senior year at University of California Berkeley. The family was taken to live in a horse stall for five months, and then to the Topaz camp, in an area of Utah plagued by dust storms and mosquitoes. In the camp she worked as a preschool teacher. On birthdays, she

Yoshiko Uchida

128

looked through old magazines for photographs of presents she would have liked—a cake, a tea set, flowers. After a year, Uchida was accepted to graduate school and allowed to leave. She went on to become an award-winning writer of children's books, including several about the internment of Japanese Americans, in the hope that our nation "will never allow another group of people in America to be sent into a desert exile ever again."

The internees met waves of hostility as they tried to resume their former lives. Many had to start all over—their properties had been seized for nonpayment of taxes or otherwise taken away.

Said one survivor, "The effect on our community was really very difficult, and it has taken me almost my whole lifetime to understand what happened, to figure out why people did what they did." Japanese Americans' fears of seeming disloyal to the US led many to believe it was safer to blend in, stay "invisible" and refrain from being politically active, she added.

After the war and Japan's defeat, the American military helped the country to rebuild. Public opinion about Japanese Americans became more positive, and in 1952 Issei were finally allowed to become citizens.

★ OTHER ENEMIES ★

America was also at war with Germany and Italy, which led to backlash against those from the two countries. But Germans and Italians here escaped wholesale incarceration—partly because their numbers were greater and their path to citizenship had been easier.

German immigrants had not been prohibited from becoming citizens, and many did so. By now they had political and economic influence, so were spared large-scale relocation and internment. Millions of German Americans were of German birth, or had at least one parent born in Germany. The United States detained a relatively small number of Germans, eleven thousand, most of them not yet citizens and most not supporters of the Nazi regime. They were forced to leave coastal areas (from which they might have collaborated with the enemy) and move to one of twenty small camps in Texas and elsewhere.

Italian immigrants had been allowed to gain citizenship during the years before the war, and by 1940 there were millions of citizens who had been born in Italy. A small number of those who weren't citizens—mostly diplomats, businessmen, and students—around two thousand, were taken into custody and detained in military camps.

Italy's surrender on September 8, 1943, resulted in

the release of most of the Italian internees by the end of that year.

★ APOLOGIES ★

The Japanese internment camps are now considered shameful and un-American.

President Gerald Ford issued a formal apology to the surviving internees in 1976, saying their incarceration was a "setback to fundamental American principles."

> "We know now what we should've known then. Not only was that evacuation wrong, but Japanese Americans were and are loyal Americans."
> —*Gerald Ford, 1976*

The Supreme Court finally declared FDR's executive order of 1942 unconstitutional in 1987. It's used as a glaring example of what happens when the United States Constitution is ignored. It followed in the worst, most bigoted strain of American tradition, along with not considering American Indians and enslaved blacks equal human beings.

In 1988, President Ronald Reagan apologized again. The survivors of the camps also received $1.6 billion in reparations ($20,000 each)—a rare concession by the American government. "Here we admit a wrong," Reagan said. "Here we reaffirm our commitment as a nation to equal justice under the law."

A 1998 mandate ruled that all students in California's public schools learn about the internment of Japanese Americans.

The federal government has never apologized to the Germans or Italians. But in 2010, thanks to a campaign by a citizen appalled by treatment of his relatives during the war, the California legislature passed a resolution apologizing for US mistreatment of Italian residents during the war.

Earl Warren, one of the forces behind the Japanese internment and who later served on the Supreme Court, felt a burden of guilt. In 1977 he wrote: "Whenever I thought of the innocent little children who were torn from home, school friends, and congenial surroundings, I was conscience-stricken. It was wrong to react so impulsively, without positive evidence of disloyalty."

CHAPTER TEN

★ ★ ★

Open Arms,
Then Closed

The end of World War II marked a whole new era in immigration: the arrival of refugees.

Refugees are those forced to leave their home country because of natural disaster, deadly persecution, or the trauma of war. Technically, America's first refugees were Quakers and Puritans, who came here in the 1600s because of religious persecution, and we have taken in many since. Even in times when nativism rules, the plight of certain groups has sometimes been so dire that they have moved the conscience of America and managed to find a safe haven here.

★ REFUGEES ★

Millions of people across Europe and other places were displaced, or lost everything, in World War II.

Meanwhile, mainland America was never invaded or heavily bombed. It emerged as a world leader and the richest nation in the world. It was in a uniquely powerful position to help, and it did with the Displaced Persons Act of 1948. This allowed refugees from war-torn Europe to start immigrating here.

After the war, most American women who had been holding down jobs while the men were off fighting went back into the home. There were jobs for nearly every man who wanted one.

Immigrant Story—Albert Einstein

Perhaps America's most famous immigrant fled here in 1933, the year Adolf Hitler came to power in Germany. Supporters helped Albert Einstein to go on with his scientific research at Princeton University. Einstein had changed how everyone saw the world with his theory of relativity. He also foresaw an end to World War II. After Hitler invaded Poland in 1939, Einstein wrote a famous letter to FDR, warning that an atom bomb was now possible, a nuclear weapon more powerful than anything ever before seen. And if America didn't start working on one, Hitler might create one first, unleashing devastation

Albert Einstein

on the rest of the world. Einstein's letter led directly
to the super-secret Manhattan Project to produce
the world's first nuclear weapon. Other refugee
scientists who contributed to work on the atom
bomb and helped America win the war were Enrico
Fermi from Italy, Leo Szilard from Hungary, and Lise
Meitner from Austria.

During the post-war years, the refugees included—
finally—some 140,000 Jewish people fleeing persecution.
These were survivors of the Holocaust, in some cases
the only surviving members of their families. They were
young, mostly between fifteen and thirty-five years old,
and had survived by hiding, avoiding imprisonment in
the concentration camps.

★ ANOTHER KIND OF WAR ★

World War II had ended, but another war began—between
the United States and the Communist Soviet Union. It

was called the Cold War because the two countries didn't fight directly. Creating an atmosphere of paranoia and distrust, the Soviet Union installed a symbolic barrier, or an "Iron Curtain," over the countries it wanted to control—Poland, Hungary, Czechoslovakia, Bulgaria, Yugoslavia, the western part of Germany, and others.

Communism terrified Americans. It went against all the liberties America stood for—it was a movement toward a society in which everything is owned in common. The way the Soviet Union imposed it was brutal and unfair, allowing for no disagreement, using force, and killing millions. But the Soviet Union had also emerged from World War II as a superpower, and America saw it as a giant threat.

Those fleeing Communist rule in Central Europe and Russia were welcome here. Hungarians, after their 1956 revolution was crushed by the Soviets, found a temporary hole in the Iron Curtain that allowed refugees to escape, bringing in thousands of new Hungarian families to the United States by 1960.

★ Immigrant Story—Sergey Brin

One of Google's founders immigrated with his family from the Soviet Union when he was six years old. Despite the Cold War, "the United

States had the courage to take me and my family in as refugees," said Sergey Brin. Sergey's father, a scientist, was stalled in his career because Soviet leaders discriminated against Jews. His mother feared their son would not be allowed to follow his dreams either. In America Sergey followed the family tradition of studying math and then computer science. Working with a friend in a rented garage, he developed a new search engine. Google's mission statement is to "organize the world's information and make it universally accessible and useful." Brin is one of the richest people in the world. "I would not be where I am today," he said, "if this was not a brave country that really stood out and spoke for liberty."

The 1959 Cuban Revolution, in which the Communist Fidel Castro took over the government, drove many who opposed him into exile. America gave permanent resident status to Cubans once they had been physically present in the United States for one year if they entered after January 1, 1959. President Lyndon Johnson welcomed them in 1965: "[Our tradition] as an asylum for the oppressed is going to be upheld."

By 1970, hundreds of thousands of Cubans had immigrated to the United States.

★ Immigrant Story—Gloria Estefan

When she was a child, Gloria Estefan fled with her family to Miami, Florida, after the Cuban Revolution. She became a citizen in 1974. After

college, she went to work as a translator and began recording albums, achieving a brilliant career as a singer. Her many awards include the Presidential Medal of Freedom for her contributions to American music, as well as the Ellis Island Medal of Honor, the highest award that can be given to a naturalized US citizen, for achievers within their own ethnic group who also exemplify American values.

Gloria Estefan

★ THE PUSH-PULL CONTINUES DURING THE COLD WAR YEARS ★

But fear caused much of the American response to the Cold War to be anti-immigrant.

In 1950, Communist North Korea invaded South Korea, starting the Korean War. America reacted by barring Communists from any country who might engage in activities "which would be prejudicial to the public interest, or would endanger the welfare or safety of the United States."

One effect was that all kinds of writers and scholars were banned from traveling to the United States because of potentially anti-American political views. Provisions that excluded immigrants with certain political beliefs weren't revoked until the Immigration Act of 1990.

At the start of World War II in 1941, those traveling to America needed an official passport issued by the United States Department of State. In response to the Cold War, even stricter laws made it illegal to enter the United States at any time without a passport. The passport requirement obviously made it harder to come here.

We made exceptions for those who wished to defect, or give up their citizenship in Communist countries, seeking political asylum here.

★ Immigrant Story—Nadia Comăneci

Nadia Comăneci, a citizen of Communist Romania, started sweeping all the awards in gymnastics at age thirteen. In 1976, Comăneci stunned the world as the youngest Olympic gymnastics all-around

champion ever, earning perfect 10 scores. She
gets credit for popularizing gymnastics around the
world. As her career wound down, the repressive
government of Romania forbade her to leave the
country. "I started to feel like a prisoner." She took
a long time to plan her escape—others before her
had died while trying. In 1989, with the help of a
Romanian American, she defected with a group
of other Romanians. Their treacherous journey—
traveling mostly at night and on foot—took her
through Hungary, Austria, and finally to the United
States, where she was welcomed. She married
American Olympic-gold-medal gymnast Bart
Conner and became a US citizen in 2001. She
is still involved with gymnastics and the Olympic
Games, as well as raising money for groups that
help Romanian children.

Immigrant Story—Martina Navratilova

Growing up in Communist Czechoslovakia,
Martina Navratilova began doing wizardly
things with a tennis ball by age four. She was
winning championships by age fifteen, and three
years later, strongly opposed to Communism, she
defected from Czechoslovakia (now known as the
Czech Republic). She asked the United States for
political asylum and was granted a green card for

temporary residency. Navratilova became a US citizen in 1981, and for forty years was considered the greatest woman tennis player in the world. She remains an activist for causes including animal rights, underprivileged children, and gay and lesbian rights.

Then, reflecting America's contradictory attitudes, came the very controversial and confusing McCarran-Walter Act, also known as the Immigration and Nationality Act of 1952.

Pat McCarran, a senator from Nevada, and Francis Walter, a Congressman from Pennsylvania, felt the greatest threat to America was Communist infiltration through immigration. McCarran warned, "We have in the United States today hard-core, indigestible blocs which have not become integrated into the American way of life, but which, on the contrary are its deadly enemies."

Their Immigration and Nationality Act of 1952 upheld the national origins quota system established by the Immigration Act of 1924, reinforcing this controversial system of immigrant selection. It renewed the ban against almost all Asians and most Jews. It barred members, former members, and associates of the Communist Party from entry.

The act defined the types of acceptable immigrants: highly educated professionals like scientists; relatives of US citizens, who were exempt from quotas and who were to be admitted without restrictions; other immigrants, not to exceed 270,000 per year; and refugees. Individuals with special skills or families already resident in the United States received precedence, a policy still in use today.

The act also allowed the government to deport immigrants or naturalized citizens suspected of engaging in subversive (Communist) activities.

★ Senator Pat McCarran, Anti-Immigrant

"I take no issue with those who would praise the contributions which have been made to our society by people of many races, of varied creeds and colors. . . . However . . . today, as never before, untold millions are storming our gates for admission and those gates are cracking under the strain. The solution of the problems of Europe and Asia will not come through a transplanting of those problems en masse to the United States. . . . I do not intend to become prophetic, but if the enemies of this legislation succeed in riddling it to pieces, or in amending it beyond recognition, they will have contributed more to promote this nation's downfall than any other group since we achieved our independence as a nation."

President Harry Truman, Pro-Immigrant

"We want to stretch out a helping hand, to save those who have managed to flee into Western Europe, to succor those who are brave enough to escape from barbarism, to welcome and restore them against the day when their countries will, as we hope, be free again. . . . In no other realm of our national life are we so hampered and stultified by the dead hand of the past, as we are in this field of immigration."

President Harry Truman

President Truman thought the new McCarran-Walter Act was discriminatory, and he vetoed it. But the law had enough support in Congress to pass over his veto.

Limited and selective immigration was considered to be the best way to ensure the preservation of national security.

Fear had won the day—for the time being.

CHAPTER ELEVEN

★ ★ ★

The Sixties Bring an Epic Change

The Cold War wasn't the only thing preoccupying Americans. Social changes, particularly among young people, were about to inspire a shift in immigration policy.

The 1960s tweaked American society in all sorts of ways. In particular, the civil rights revolution was effective in finally changing the laws that held back African Americans from the rights of full citizenship.

As a result, many politicians were taking a more critical look at our restrictive immigration policies, which were seeming . . . actually, not very American. With America now spearheading the fight against Communism, it could not afford criticism of its racist immigration limits.

★ PEOPLE BEHIND THE CHANGE ★

Years after World War II had made America the world leader, the country was enjoying an era of prosperity in the 1960s. Everyone wanted to come here, and we were feeling charitable. Immigration wasn't seen as being as much of a threat as in other eras. Some felt guilty for past intolerance, seeing it as racism, and began trying to change American policy.

President John F. Kennedy, in a 1963 speech to the American Committee on Italian Migration, called the system of quotas "nearly intolerable."

After JFK's assassination later that year, two men in Congress—Representative Emanuel Celler and Senator Philip Hart—made it their mission to change the law. Their biggest influence was former President Truman, who had directed a committee that produced a pro-immigrant report called *Whom We Shall Welcome*. Hart and Celler used it as a blueprint to draw up a new system that would aim for more fairness.

Hart and Celler

Representative Emanuel Celler of New York City and Senator Philip Hart of Michigan represented areas with lots of immigrants. Celler expressed concerns that the quota system heavily favored immigration from Northern and Western Europe,

145

creating resentment against the United States in other parts of the world. He felt the law implied that Americans thought of people from Eastern Europe as less desirable and people from Asia as inferior to those of European descent.

Congress debated mightily. The person most responsible for fighting for the law and steering it through the Senate was young Massachusetts senator Edward Kennedy, part of the Kennedy political dynasty. He dedicated his effort to the memory of his late brother, JFK, working hard to counter the fear that this law would have a negative impact.

Senator Edward M. Kennedy

The 1965 Immigration and Naturalization Act, also known as the Hart-Celler Act, passed with overwhelming majorities. Some seventy percent of the public approved. The law was seen as an extension of the civil rights movement that was gaining equal rights for African Americans.

President Lyndon Johnson signed the act into law at a ceremony held under the Statue of Liberty. He declared that "the harsh injustice" of the national-origins quota system had been "abolished." He considered it a jewel in the crown of his Great Society goals—reforms designed to eliminate poverty and racial injustice with spending programs to address rural poverty, urban problems, and education.

⭐ LBJ

"We must also lift by legislation the bars of discrimination against those who seek entry into our country, particularly those who have much needed skills and those joining their families. In establishing preferences, a nation that was built by the immigrants of all lands can ask those who now seek admission: 'What can you do for our country?' But we should not be asking: 'In what country were you born?'"

—*President Lyndon B. Johnson, 1964*

President Lyndon B. Johnson

"This bill says simply that from this day forth, those wishing to immigrate to America shall be admitted on the basis of their skills and their close relationships to those already here. The fairness of this standard is so self-evident that we may well wonder that it has not always been applied."

—*President Lyndon B. Johnson, 1965*

★ WHAT THE HART-CELLER ACT DID ★

At long last, it ended the quota system that favored certain European immigrants. It eliminated national origin, race, and ancestry as bases for immigration.

Instead, it created a seven-category preference system, which gave priority to relatives of US citizens, legal permanent residents, and to professionals and other individuals with specialized skills in occupations deemed critical by the US Department of Labor. These "special immigrants" included ministers, former employees of the US government, and foreign medical school graduates. Immediate relatives and "special immigrants" were not subject to numerical restrictions.

In essence, the Hart-Celler Act leveled the immigration playing field, giving a nearly equal shot to newcomers from every corner of the world.

> "The Immigration Act of 1965 did nothing less than ensure that America remained a land of diversity whose identity rested on a set of political principles rather than blood and soil nationalism."
> —historian Randall B. Woods, 2007

When the law took effect in the drama-packed year of 1968, some of the first to take advantage were from Italy, Greece, and Poland. These were places that had labored under very small quotas—from a few hundred to a few thousand.

The measure had not been particularly intended to stimulate immigration from Asia, the Middle East, Africa, and elsewhere in the developing world. But it did, and within two years, immigrants began to hail from Korea, China, India, the Philippines, and Pakistan, as well as countries in Africa. They also came from Mexico, South and Central America, the Caribbean islands of the West Indies, and other areas of political instability.

Chinese immigrant children

By 2000, immigration had returned to its 1900 volume. With the largest wave in its history, the United States once again became a nation formed and transformed by immigrants. We had African doctors, Indian engineers, Chinese computer programmers, and much more.

The 1965 law had the effect of changing the face of America. Public approval of the law has shifted over the decades—sinking to a low in the 1990s, rising again to a majority in 2014, becoming a topic of great debate today.

Immigrant Story—Jerry Yang

Jerry Yang left Taiwan with his family when his mother moved to San Jose in 1978. He was ten and knew only one word in English: shoe. He went on to earn several college degrees, becoming an expert on a new thing—the internet. He founded Yahoo!, a pioneering search engine, in 1994. He has been called one of the top one hundred innovators in the world under the age of thirty-five. He is currently worth $2.7 billion.

★ SOME EXAMPLES OF CHANGES AFTER 1965 ★

Before 1965, quotas strictly limited immigration from the Philippines. After 1965, significant Filipino immigration began. By 2011, four percent of the foreign-born population was Filipino.

In 1950, the invasion of South Korea by Communist North Korea started the Korean War and left a war-ravaged Korea behind. There had been little Korean immigration to the United States due to the quota system in place. Significant South Korean immigration began after 1965, totaling one million by 2017. Since 2006, a few hundred refugees have defected here from Communist North Korea.

Black immigrants also began to arrive, first from the Caribbean Islands, then Haiti, Grenada, Ghana, Nigeria, Jamaica, Senegal, and elsewhere in Africa.

★ Immigrant Story—Chimamanda Ngozi Adichie

Chimamanda Adichie is a Nigerian citizen but has permanent resident status (permission to live and work) in the United States. Back in Nigeria, she did very well in school, and anyone who did so was pressured into becoming a doctor. She started studying medicine—and she was miserable. Her heart's desire was to be a writer. So she got a scholarship and left, moving to live with her American-born sister. Today she is a prominent contributor to African literature, traveling to teach around the world.

⭐ Immigrant Story—Elon Musk

ElonMusk got interested in computers while growing up in South Africa. He was a huge

reader, especially of Isaac Asimov (a fellow immigrant, from Russia). Musk moved to the US when he was twenty-four years old and became a citizen in 2002. He was an ambitious inventor, and he founded SolarCity (one of the

Elon Musk

largest providers of solar power systems), Tesla (fabulous electric cars, named for scientist Nikola Tesla—a fellow immigrant, from Serbia), and X.com (which became PayPal). He plans to establish a human colony on Mars, and is the one of the wealthiest people in the world. According to Musk, the United States is "the greatest country that has ever existed on Earth," as well as "the greatest force for good of any country that's ever been."

The new law paved the way for many South Asian families, from India and elsewhere, to immigrate. Today Indian Americans have the highest median income of any ethnic group in the United States, many with careers as doctors or other highly educated professionals.

★ Asian American

By 2013, Asian Americans were the fast-growing group of immigrants, many with a goal of attending American universities. Asian Americans, as a group, are not all alike. Besides China and Japan, they come here from India, Vietnam, the Philippines, Korea, Laos, Cambodia, Tibet, and others — countries that are all very different from each other. Most of these immigrants do not consider themselves "Asian American" until they move here and receive the label. *Oriental*, a descriptive word used to describe people in the past, is now considered to be a racist, derogatory term.

★ WOMEN AGAIN TAKE THE LEAD ★

After the new law, many more single women immigrated than ever before, taking advantage of this opportunity. In America they were able to earn relatively high wages, working at all levels of employment. In some groups the majority of immigrants were women.

Women immigrants became the pioneers in making connections, getting established, and then working toward reuniting their families.

⭐ Why Nurses?

Over the years, as America endured a nursing shortage—American women were drawn to jobs with less stress and higher pay—we made it easy for experienced Filipino nurses to immigrate here. They could make much more money than they could in their home country and were able to send money home to support their families. Filipino Americans continue to fill many health-care positions today.

★ MORE REFUGEES ★

The 1965 law meant that America could do more to extend a hand to refugees fleeing crises.

In 1980, about 125,000 Cubans fled economic hardship, arriving in Florida in packed boats. The influx, known as the Mariel Boatlift, was controversial, as it

Mariel Boatlift

turned out many had been released from prisons or mental health hospitals.

Also controversial were the refugees who came after the Vietnam War ended in 1975.

When Saigon fell to the Communist forces of North Vietnam and the United States prepared to pull out its forces, leaders felt a duty to help allies left behind. Among the first targets of the new regime would surely be anyone who had helped American forces, or who was married to an American or had family living in America.

But many Americans were fiercely opposed to letting in Vietnamese asylum-seekers, frightened about allowing another Asian group in, and worried about their effect on the economy and the housing market. Polls showed 37 percent in favor of helping the refugees, with 49 percent against and 14 percent uncertain.

Vietnamese refugees

Vietnamese refugees suffered tremendous hardship in escaping. They were called "boat people" because they traveled through dangerous waters to camps in Southeast Asia and Hong Kong and from there to other countries. They paid outrageous fees and risked attack by pirates, kidnapping, and death at sea.

President Jimmy Carter

In 1979 President Jimmy Carter insisted that taking them in was the right thing to do. He announced that he would double the number of refugees from Vietnam, plus nearby Cambodia and Laos, from seven thousand per month to fourteen thousand.

Polls showed that 62 percent of Americans disapproved.

Carter did it anyway.

Vietnamese immigrants made it here and began climbing the economic ladder. Many were welcomed through Camp Pendleton near San Diego, leading to that city becoming one of the most open to refugees.

Today the 1.3 million immigrants from Vietnam and their children, along with their culture and cuisine, are part of the American mosaic.

★ Refugees

"By protecting refugees from persecution, we honor our nation's finest traditions."
—*Senator Edward Kennedy, 2009*

"Refugees, many of whom arrive having lost everything, have become some of the most resilient . . . and devoted citizens we have."
—*Senator John Kerry, 2010*

In the years after the 1979 Iranian Revolution, in which the pro-Western government was overthrown, America accepted hundreds of thousands of refugees from Iran in search of social, political, and religious freedom. They settled mostly in Washington, DC; Los Angeles; San Francisco; and areas of New York. Because the landscape and the climate reminded them of home, Southern California has the nation's highest concentration of Iranian Americans, in areas known as Little Tehran or Persian Square. Today Iranian Americans are among the best educated and most financially successful communities in the United States.

Throughout the 1980s and 1990s, under first Carter and then Reagan, America took in Central Americans. Hundreds of thousands, perhaps as many as a million, came from El Salvador, Guatemala, and Nicaragua. They were fleeing north from civil war, state-sponsored murders, natural disasters, and economic devastation. They settled in Los Angeles, Miami, and other big cities, creating new lives for themselves and making contributions to American culture, especially in food and music.

In the early 1990s, during the Bosnian War—part of the fallout from the breakup of Yugoslavia—some forty thousand traumatized Bosnians fled here. Today, thanks to active local resettlement agencies and several Bosnian families already living there, the largest Bosnian community outside of Europe is in St. Louis, Missouri, with other communities in Chicago, Detroit, and elsewhere.

At several points in Haiti's troubled history, many Haitians—especially professionals, the middle class, and students—left to escape an oppressive government, natural disasters, and economic hardship. Numbering approximately one million, they settled in Florida, New York, and elsewhere.

The overwhelming majority of refugees have been through significant trauma. They're grateful to America and proud to be here. People who had been doctors, translators, or engineers in their home countries are often anxious to contribute any way they can, even scrubbing pots and cleaning hotel rooms.

★ A CLUSTERING PHENOMENON ★

As the face of America changed after 1965, it is interesting to note that certain immigrant groups chose certain industries. Why?

Immigrants often live and socialize with those who are similar to them. When they arrive, they tend to stay with relatives or friends, people with familiar customs and language. Friends teach skills to friends and help them get jobs, which can lead those in a community to work in a certain industry, continuing the success of generations that came before them.

So it happens that certain nationalities dominate certain industries. Greek immigrants own more restaurants than other immigrants, Vietnamese are more likely to own nail salons, Koreans are more apt to run dry-cleaners, and Yemeni immigrants are seventy-five times more likely than other immigrants to own grocery stores. The motel business draws Indians from the Gujarat state on the western border of India—they're 108 times more likely than other immigrants to run motels. Entry-level jobs, such as driving a taxi or cooking in a restaurant, tend to be dominated by certain groups as well.

The trend is most noticeable in careers that lend themselves to self-employment, a trademark of many immigrants. Anticipating facing job discrimination in many fields, many immigrants prefer to be their own bosses, using the skills they've brought with them.

For example, 45 percent of Korean men are self-employed, compared to 15 percent of the male immigrant population in general. For the self-employed, advice and support is critical, and fellow immigrants are there to help. Business owners are likely to hire fellow immigrants to work for them, acting as mentors. They're creating a pipeline in which owners are able to pass their businesses down to their children and grandchildren.

> "Since the beginning of the great unfinished symphony that is our American experiment, time and time again, immigrants get the job done."
>
> —playwright Lin-Manuel Miranda (whose heritage is Puerto Rican and Mexican), creator of the Broadway musical Hamilton

CHAPTER TWELVE

★ ★ ★

The History of Mexicans in America from 1846 Onward

After the Mexican-American War ended in 1848, an arbitrary border was born. America won the war and promptly swallowed, or took over, present-day Texas, Arizona, California, New Mexico, and parts of what would become other states.

Most of the eighty thousand Mexican residents of those areas chose to stay, becoming the country's first Mexican Americans.

★ UP AND DOWN ★

Since then, Mexican immigration waves have been more up and down than just about any other nation's.

With our southern border so easy to cross that it

was basically porous, American employers saw Mexico as a convenient source of labor. The number of Mexican workers in the country has fluctuated according to the demands of American employers.

⭐ Anti-Mexican

"In the case of the Mexican, he is less desirable as a citizen than as a laborer."
—1911 US Immigration Commission

Early in the 1900s America called upon Mexican workers when Japanese immigration decreased and cheap labor was needed in agriculture, railroad building, and mining.

During the prosperous times of the Roaring Twenties, hundreds of thousands of Mexicans were welcomed here to work. When the Depression crushed the economy and jobs were scarce, millions were deported, by force if necessary, to resume their old lives throughout the 1930s.

With the start of World War II, with so many American men fighting overseas, the country brought in millions of Mexican guest workers during the 1940s to fill labor shortages in agriculture. It was called the Bracero Program—bracero meaning someone who works with his arms.

Bracero workers

Then, after the war, came Operation Wetback—an outdated, insulting, and racist term referring to workers literally getting their backs wet as they crossed the Rio Grande. An official declared that the United States was actually being invaded by an "alarming, ever-increasing flood tide." In 1954, over a million immigrants were picked up by the Border Patrol and forced to return to Mexico. Meanwhile, immigration never ceased— Mexican laborers were still needed. Operation Wetback was considered a failure.

★ **Immigrant Story—Amelia Morán Ceja**

Amelia Morán Ceja's family migrated to California in the 1950s to work in the vineyards. They started out picking grapes and cleaning wineries and moved on to become vineyard managers. Ceja joined them in 1967, working in the vineyards after school. While studying history and literature at the University of California-San Diego, she began creating authentic Mexican cuisine wine dinners for friends. She made videos and appeared on TV to demonstrate her recipes. In 1999 she cofounded Ceja Vineyards in Napa and Sonoma counties— the first Mexican American woman to be president of a California winery. The California legislature recognized Ceja as Woman of the Year in 2005 for "breaking the glass ceiling in a very competitive business." She champions migrant workers: "Even today, the farmworkers are invisible, and we need to advocate for them. Through our wines we are paying homage to the true artists of wine—the workers." Hers is one of at least five families who started out as migrant grape pickers and now own their own wineries.

★ NEEDING DOCUMENTS ★

With a border so easy to cross, no quotas had been imposed on legal Mexican immigration, so by 1963, more than fifty thousand Mexicans were immigrating each year. There were so many legal ways to enter the country that illegal immigration was virtually unknown. Then, in 1965, the US ended the Bracero Program and for the first time began to impose quotas on Mexican immigration.

But the demand for Mexican labor remained as strong as ever. And so began the era of "undocumented" migration: people coming here without the proper legal documents. (American Indians, of course, might consider everyone who arrived after them undocumented.)

Immigrant Story—Alfredo Quiñones-Hinojosa

Desperate to escape poverty in his hometown of Mexicali, Mexico, Alfredo hopped a border fence and slipped into America at age nineteen. He started out as a migrant farm worker, then took night classes while working as a welder. He was able to win legal status through an amnesty program—it allowed residency visas (green cards) to immigrants who could prove they'd been working regularly. He became a citizen at age twenty-seven. He graduated from the University of California, went on to medical school, and today is a brain surgeon at Johns Hopkins University Hospital.

The term illegal immigration hasn't been used in most of our history. With certain exceptions, immigration was a legal, positive thing. After 1965, this changed. Large numbers of Mexicans and other Latinos came across the easily crossed southern border without papers, and fear grew. The issue of illegal immigration was born and soon turned into a hot potato.

But even as millions of Mexicans entered the US illegally, millions also returned to the homeland to find work or be with their families. About 85 percent of new entries were offset by departures. Consequently, the growth of the undocumented population was slow.

From 1986 to 2000, due to the North American Free Trade Agreement (opening up trade between the US, Canada, and Mexico), trade with Mexico increased eightfold. The permanent undocumented population exploded, and the border became increasingly militarized. Border arrests of undocumented immigrants rose to 1.7 million in 1986 from fifty-five thousand in 1965.

Before 1986, by far the majority of Mexicans who entered the US settled in California, Texas, or Illinois. More than two-thirds entered through either the San Diego–Tijuana entry point (the most frequently crossed border in the world) or the El Paso–Juarez entry point. As the US blockaded those areas, undocumented migrants found new ways in—and new places to settle.

★ Mexican Immigration Pro and Con

"Our largest source of immigrants is Mexico . . . The number of Mexican immigrants who want to bring the Mexican system of law and government to the United States is minuscule. The overwhelming majority of Latin—and Asian—immigrants are interested primarily in work."

—Michael Barone, The New Americans, 2001

"Mexican immigration is a unique, disturbing, and looming challenge to our cultural integrity, our national identity, and potentially to our future as a country."

—political scientist Samuel Huntington, 2000

In 1986, President Ronald Reagan signed the controversial Immigration Reform and Control Act (IRCA). For the first time, it created penalties for employers who hired illegal immigrants. But IRCA was also projected to give amnesty, or a pardon, to about one million workers in the country illegally. In practice, amnesty was granted for about three million immigrants already in the United States. Most were from Mexico.

★ Immigrant Story—José Quiñonez

After their mother died, nine-year-old José Quiñonez and his siblings left Mexico without documents in 1980 to live with relatives in California. The children worked at a flea market to get money for food. Six years later Quiñonez got amnesty through the Immigration Reform and Control Act. He studied hard and earned a master's degree in public affairs from Princeton University. He wanted to help other immigrants and went on to found the Mission Asset Fund, in which a group of immigrants provide interest-free loans and pay one another back gradually. "We help hardworking immigrants to build and develop their financial security by first acknowledging their financial savvy." In 2016, he won a MacArthur Fellowship, known as a "genius grant," in honor of his work in connecting low-income immigrants to mainstream financial services. "I wanted to bring my story out of my immigrant experience to tell a different narrative about who we are as a people and what we want to do in this country."

In 1994, California voters adopted a harsh referendum, Proposition 187, denying state services to undocumented immigrants, including public education and health care. The idea was to make life so unpleasant for immigrants that they would leave on their own, or self-deport. The proposition was struck down by the courts as unconstitutional and discriminatory.

And so the ups and downs of Mexican immigration waves continued.

CHAPTER THIRTEEN

★ ★ ★

Helping Children

What about children? For most of its history, America has often showed compassion to unaccompanied minors—from the most famous, Annie Moore, onward. Especially during times of crisis, America has given a helping hand to children traveling alone.

Ellis Island officials looked out for children. There was a playground with swings, slides, and a sandbox. A dozen women known as matrons played games and sang songs with them. The Red Cross brought in a radio. A schoolroom was eventually installed. Unaccompanied children were never turned away but detained until someone came forward to speak for them—their parents, private citizens, a church, or an immigrant aid society.

If they lacked an adult to travel with, desperate children occasionally took matters into their own hands and stowed away on boats coming to Ellis Island. We don't know how many, but when they were found, they weren't sent back.

★ Immigrant Story—Henry Armetta

The most famous Ellis Island stowaway was a fourteen-year-old Italian boy, Henry Armetta. Once he was in New York, a local Italian man offered to sponsor him. Armetta delivered groceries, made pizza, pressed pants, and did whatever he could to get by until he got the attention of someone who championed his acting ability. He went on to Hollywood fame, from 1915 to 1946, appearing in at least 150 movies with icons like the Marx Brothers and Judy Garland.

Children orphaned by war or famine have sometimes been sponsored by religious groups or other charities to come to safety in America. The Orphan Train Movement was a program operating between 1854 and 1929, relocating about two hundred thousand orphaned, abandoned, or homeless children to rural areas of the Midwest.

World War II put countless children in peril. Some groups stepped up to help. One Thousand Children, for example, was an informal network of organizations and concerned people rescuing Jewish children from Nazi-controlled Europe. Operating from 1933 to 1948, the group shepherded the children to America a dozen at a time, finding them homes with Jewish foster families. Most of the children became the only members of their families to survive the Holocaust.

After the revolution that brought Communist Fidel Castro to power in 1959, Cuban parents were alarmed. They feared that he was going to close schools and send children to camps where they would be indoctrinated, or brainwashed. From 1960 to 1962, Operation Pedro Pan helped fourteen thousand children from Cuba get to the United States. It was organized by Cuban parents, the Catholic Church, and the American government.

★ OPERATION BABYLIFT ★

Another rescue operation took place in Vietnam. As the Vietnam War ended in 1975 and the country was in chaos, with thousands trying to evacuate, President Gerald Ford announced a new program. Operation Babylift entailed the emergency evacuation of three thousand orphans to America, where they were adopted.

"This is the least we can do," said Ford, who personally helped some of the tiny refugees off the planes. Nurses made bassinets for the babies out of cardboard boxes that had held produce. "Everyone was extremely

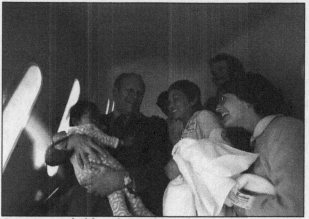

Operation Babylift with Gerald Ford

hospitable and welcoming," said one of the evacuees as an adult.

★ Immigrant Story—Andy Hoang

Andy Hoang really was a baby—just three weeks old when Operation Babylift started. His mother made the wrenching decision to get Andy out of Vietnam and to safety with an aunt in the United States. She planned to put him on the first plane out. But at the last minute, she changed her mind, unwilling to part with her newborn. That plane crashed in a rice paddy—killing seventy-eight children. The Hoang family, with Andy, was able to get out together on a later flight to a refugee camp in Arkansas. From there they went to Camp Pendleton. "The reception we got when we first arrived in this country is the opposite of what is going on today," said Hoang. "Everybody was extremely hospitable and welcoming, especially the service members at Pendleton." Hoang grew up in Orange County and became a vice president at California State University, Long Beach. He makes trips back to Vietnam and Cambodia to build orphanages.

★ THE LOST BOYS ★

In 1989, a civil war in Sudan killed millions and created a horrifying humanitarian crisis. Boys as young as six or seven were being forced to fight in the army as child soldiers. A rescue effort began in 2001. Those who examined them reported that the boys were extremely malnourished and more war-traumatized than any children they had seen.

America took in some four thousand so-called Lost Boys of Sudan—refugees, orphans, or those separated from their families. Through the work of church groups and government agencies, they settled in Omaha, Nebraska, and dozens of other cities.

They faced numerous adjustments, including snow for those placed in wintery climates. Said one Sudanese Lost Boy in Michigan, "We feel very happy. The only problem here is the coolness." Another said that it took him about a year to "see what America is really like, that it's entirely dependent on you to make your life what you want it to be."

⭐ Immigrant Story—Alephonsion Deng

The most famous of the Lost Boys is Alephonsion Deng. In 1989, when Alephonsion was seven, his village in Southern Sudan was attacked by government troops. To avoid capture into the army he ran into the night with many other young boys. "We ran in different directions not knowing where we are going. We gathered some fruits for our breakfast and lunch. We, little boys, were so messy, all chaos and cries filled the dark fiercely lightless night." Without food, water, shoes, or parents, he began a journey of a thousand miles and five years. Fleeing war, starvation, and lions and crocodiles, he finally reached a refugee camp in Kenya. In 1999 the United States welcomed Alephonsion as one of the Lost Boys of Sudan. "I had this image of the United States as a land of dreams, a land of opportunity, a land of hope. And that turned out to be true." His first job was as a clerk and stocker at Ralph's grocery store in San Diego. His adjustment was difficult. "Always the outsider who was ready to fight, I existed in a cloud of anger and depression." Writing helped him work through his trauma. He went on to coauthor a book about his harrowing experience: *They Poured Fire on Us from the Sky: The True Story of Three Lost Boys of Sudan*. When he's not speaking around the country about his extraordinary story of survival, he works in the medical records department at Kaiser Permanente and plays bass in the San Diego–based band Thong Jieng.

CHAPTER FOURTEEN

★ ★ ★

The Food Chapter

Immigrants have made one key contribution to America after another. You might listen to reggae from Jamaica or K-pop from South Korea, or read Japanese manga, or practice yoga from India. Or you might have gone to kindergarten or gotten gifts from Santa Claus (both German ideas).

But the contribution many prize the most is food. Immigrants who have starred in this arena have some of the most dramatic stories of struggle and survival.

American cuisine is part of the American dream. It takes in flavors from all over the world, with a constant stimulation to our taste buds and our culture. The food brought here by immigrants is often

Americanized—made a bit blander. But whether you prefer Cambodian or Ethiopian, Vietnamese or Serbian, Middle Eastern hummus and kabobs or Mexican chili rellenos,our choices are uniquely numerous and help to make America the place that it is.

★ Immigrant Story—David Tran

David Tran, the founder of the company that makes Sriracha Hot Chili Sauce, is a Vietnamese immigrant. In 1978 Tran, along with his family and more than three thousand others, boarded a freighter and escaped to Hong Kong. From there he was taken into the United States as a refugee, along with hundreds of thousands of other refugees who he knew would be homesick for the flavors they loved. Back home he'd been a peppery-hot-sauce maker, spicing up the popular national dish of pho. He began making his own sauce here, using peppers grown on a farm near Los Angeles. Sriracha became enormously popular, even outside the Vietnamese community, and today sells out faster than his company can make it.

★ FROM GERMAN TO CHINESE ★

Germans have contributed perhaps the most popular foods to America—hot dogs, hamburgers, sausages, and more. Chili powder was invented by a German American in 1897 to use in making Mexican food in the United States. Picnic is a German word. For a long time, any foreign food was presumed to be German. All these years later, we tend to simply consider it American.

★ Immigrant Story—Henry John Heinz

Henry John Heinz was the son of German immigrants who came to America in their twenties. He started selling produce from his mother's garden at the age of eight, and by the time he was twelve, he was raising crops on his own piece of land. He grew up to found Heinz, a national company that makes food products, in 1869. He started with ketchup and went on to horseradish, lots of pickles, olive oil, peanut butter, baby food, soups, and all kinds of prepared foods—the

Henry John Heinz, middle, bottom row.

famous "57 Varieties" (though technically the
company made more—he just liked that number).
The company grew to more than twenty food
processing plants during his lifetime. Besides
championing safe and sanitary food preparation,
Heinz was unusually nice to his employees—with
free medical care, a swimming pool and gym,
hot showers, libraries and free concerts, even
weekly manicures for the women. Today his is one
of the world's most successful companies, with
manufacturing plants around the word—a classic
American success story.

Chinese immigrants had enormous impact on food
history early on—in part because of the prejudice toward
them. Officials feared that Chinese workers accepting
lower wages in more lucrative fields, like mining, would
threaten the jobs of American men, but they were okay
with letting them work less desirable jobs, like cooking.
Getting into the United States became much easier if
one entered as a small business owner, particularly as a
restaurant owner. Whole communities would pool their
money, becoming restaurant partners and creating a multiplicity of Chinese restaurants.

The first Chinese workers brought in chop suey,
chow mein, egg foo young, egg rolls, and plum sauce—all
popular but adapted to be less spicy for American tastes.

When the Chinese were banned from immigrating in 1882, their food contributions stalled. Once restrictions were eased in 1965, a much wider variety of cuisine was brought to the US, with Sichuan peppers and scrumptious regional dishes.

Today, in most American cities, there seems to be a Chinese restaurant on every corner.

★ Immigrant Story—Dr. Yamei Kin

As a two-year-old orphan in China, Yamei Kin was taken in by the family of a medical missionary from Philadelphia. She spent parts of her childhood in Japan and the United States. In 1888 she became the first Chinese woman to earn a medical degree in the United States, from the Women's Medical College in New York (founded by Dr. Elizabeth Blackwell, also an immigrant). Kin moved to San Francisco and began lecturing around the country about Chinese culture, women, medicine, and food, like soy sauce and cakes made from soybeans—that is, tofu. Tofu was bland, but depending on how it was cooked, could mimic any flavor. It was a promising, nutritious alternative to meat, and during World War I Kin tried to make it widely available to American troops suffering from meat shortages. Her attempt failed for lack of soybeans being grown in quantity in America then, but she gets the credit for introducing tofu to the United States. It became trendy in the 1960s and is now a supermarket staple.

★ AND MUCH MORE ★

As Jewish immigrants to New York City became more prosperous, they began eating out, and thus was born the New York Jewish deli. Its delicacies—corned beef and pastrami sandwiches on rye bread, smoked fish, chicken noodle soup, cheese blintzes, and many others—became universally popular.

Those tasty, microwavable turnovers known as Hot Pockets? They were invented in the 1970s by Paul and David Merage, two Jewish Iranian brothers who immigrated to the United States from Tehran.

Immigrant Story—Ranji Smile

Ranji Smile was perhaps the first celebrity chef. A Muslim chef from Karachi, India, he moved to London and then to the fanciest restaurants of New York in 1899. He introduced Americans to Indian curries, and by 1907 he was touring the nation, performing cooking demonstrations at department stores and food halls. Fans, particularly women, were dazzled. "A Chef from India, Women Go Wild over Him," read one headline. But in 1929, after working here for thirty years, he left after a Supreme Court ruling denied citizenship to East Indians on the grounds that they weren't white. No further records of his life remain, but Indian restaurants became established in New York and moved throughout the country.

Garlic spiked in popularity after four million Italians came to the United States between 1880 and 1920. At first, the pungent plant was viewed as alien and off-putting, way too "foreign." Today, garlic might be the most frequently used flavor in American food.

★ Immigrant Story—Roy Choi

Roy Choi's family came from Seoul, South Korea, in 1972, when he was two. His favorite childhood memory is shaping dumplings as an eight-year-old at his family's Korean restaurant in southern California. His mother made kimchi that was so popular that the family packaged it and sold it locally. In his twenties he became obsessed with cooking, working at the best restaurants as a chef. Today he runs several popular restaurants fusing Korean and Mexican cooking, but is most famous for turning food trucks into gourmet places to eat. *Time* magazine has twice included Choi in their list of the hundred most influential people in the world.

⭐ Immigrant Story—Reuben and Rose Mattus

Reuben Mattus was born in Poland to Jewish parents, coming to America through Ellis Island. He moved to Brooklyn in 1921 as a child, working in his family's ice cream business by age ten. Rose Vesel, born in England to Jewish parents, arrived the same year, at age five. After she finished high school, she worked as a bookkeeper in the Mattus ice cream business. Once the two married, they came up with a whole new kind of ice cream—denser, with natural ingredients, high in butterfat. They called it Häagen-Dazs. In 1961 they launched a company, working together to develop delicious new flavors and market them. Eventually they sold the company for $70 million.

★ CAN FOOD BE MORE THAN FOOD? ★

With constant influences from newcomers, American cuisine is constantly evolving in its ingredients, flavors, and ideas from every corner of the globe.

⭐ Mexican Food

"I think it's the most undervalued, under-appreciated world cuisine with tremendous, tremendous potential. These are in many cases really complex, wonderful sauces; particularly from

Oaxaca, for instance, that date back from before Europe. I'm very excited about the possibilities for that cuisine, and I think we should pay more attention to it, learn more about it, and value it more."

—*American chef Anthony Bourdain, 2017*

And yet foods, like everything else about immigrants, have been resented. Long before Pearl Harbor, Japanese restaurants encountered prejudice. When we were at war with Germany during the World Wars, sauerkraut became "liberty cabbage" and hamburgers became "liberty steaks," to protest their German origins. East Indians were mocked for the intensity of their spices. As recently as a few generations ago, Italian foods like garlic and Parmesan cheese were treated with huge suspicion. "Garlic eaters" was an insulting term for Italian immigrants.

★ Immigrant Story—Hamdi Ulukaya

Hamdi Ulukaya, a Turkish immigrant of Kurdish descent, was born into a family that owned a sheep and goat farm, where they made cheese and yogurt. He came to the United States fleeing oppression and wanting to study English and take business courses. He started a small feta cheese factory in 2002, then took out a loan

Hamdi Ulukaya

to buy a large abandoned yogurt factory. By 2011, his Chobani yogurt had become the top-selling brand in America, popularizing Greek-style yogurt and creating a yogurt empire. A passionate advocate for immigrants, he employs hundreds of refugees from Africa as well as Iraq, Afghanistan, and Turkey in his factories. He pays them well and brings in translators to help them. "The minute a refugee has a job, that's the minute they stop being a refugee." Worth almost $2 billion, he has promised to give away a majority of his fortune to assist refugees.

★ Restaurant Workers

"Restaurants embody the American Dream like no other industry. They're often the employer of choice for immigrants who come to America in search of new opportunities. The relationship benefits both sides: Immigrants gain valuable job experience and immediate access to opportunities, and restaurateurs can fill positions at every level. Over the next decade, restaurants will likely create more jobs than the US-born workforce can fill."

—*National Restaurant Association statement*

But today, even with nativist attitudes, food can be immune to prejudice. It's hard to imagine banning a cuisine based on its country of origin. With those fighting for the rights of immigrants, food could actually help by being a unifying force. Those who demonize unseen, faceless foreigners have a harder time demonizing tasty treats that tickle our taste buds.

Meanwhile, American food remains the most diverse in the world—thanks to the contributions from immigrants.

In terms of food, the country actually is a melting pot.

CHAPTER FIFTEEN

★ ★ ★

The Attacks of 9/11 and Immigration

In the years before September 11, 2001, attitudes toward immigration tended to be big-hearted.

One of the founding principles of the United States was that anyone could move here. We needed new immigrants to build a new nation, and we met them with open arms and a spotlit statue inscribed with welcoming words. With notable exceptions based on fear and racism, the waves of immigration basically remained high. Over the centuries, as America has flourished into a world leader, its spirit has moved more and more toward generosity and compassion.

In the Senate in 2001, John McCain from Arizona and Edward Kennedy from Massachusetts were cosponsoring a bill to make immigration policy more fair.

President George W. Bush was even hinting at a startling new development. He was planning a general amnesty, a pardon for immigrants: "The United States is a nation of immigrants. . . . The administration believes that legal immigrants should be greeted with open arms, rather than endless lines."

With a suddenness that shocked the world, all of this changed on September 11, 2001. The United States was attacked by foreign terrorists. Surpassing the attack on Pearl Harbor in 1941, 9/11 was the worst attack ever on American soil, killing almost three thousand people.

★ AMERICAN RESPONSE TO 9/11 ★

That day jolted the country in multiple ways, and one of its most profound effects was on immigration.

The nineteen Muslim men who carried out the attack were not immigrants trying to apply for citizenship; they were citizens from four Middle Eastern countries: Saudi Arabia, the United Arab Emirates, Lebanon, and Egypt. They were here legally on temporary tourist and student visas from the Immigration and Naturalization Service (INS).

Meanwhile, one-fifth of the almost three thousand people killed that day were immigrants from China, Cuba, Mexico, Syria, Guatemala, Turkey, and dozens of other countries. In a tragic way, the deaths represented the unique inclusiveness of America.

Americans were devastated and frightened, and that fear and desire to protect its citizens are what led to many laws that constricted immigration policies

Six weeks after the attacks came the USA PATRIOT Act, an effort to bolster the security of the country. USA PATRIOT stood for "Uniting and Strengthening America by Providing Appropriate Tools Required to Intercept and Obstruct Terrorism." Among other provisions, the Patriot Act greatly expanded the government's power to arrest and detain immigrants indefinitely without charging them. The act was, ironically, written by a Vietnamese immigrant.

After the passage of the Homeland Security Act in 2002, the government poured vast amounts of money into funding a new department. The Department of Homeland Security was created to deal with terrorism, border security, and more. Its goal was to prevent and respond to emergencies within our borders, particularly acts of terrorism. Its realm expanded to include matters related to immigration and customs. The INS, which had been in operation since 1933, was folded into the Department of Homeland Security in 2003. As the more powerful Immigration and Customs Enforcement (ICE) took over, deportations soared.

Local police were now required to share the fingerprints of those they arrested, even for minor traffic offenses, with Homeland Security. When the prints were run through a database and an immigration hold turned up, police could detain the arrested person until federal immigration authorities arrived. The effect was to turn local police officers into immigration agents.

Immigration rules became much stricter, more focused on keeping out terrorists than on welcoming newcomers.

★ BACKLASH AGAINST IMMIGRANTS ★

The attacks of 9/11 immediately provoked a backlash against certain communities that had been here all along—Arab, South Asian, Muslim, Hindu, Sikh. In 2001 the number of hate crimes against Muslims increased tenfold from the previous year. Those who could not distinguish between nationalities and religions struck out violently and indiscriminately. One of the first hate crimes to take place in the days following 9/11 was the murder of Balbir Singh Sodhi, an Indian Sikh misidentified as a Muslim.

Over the next twenty months, no more foreign terrorism took place. But about 760 immigrants, some documented, some not, were rounded up. They were either deported or held in the Guantanamo Bay military

Guantanamo Bay

prison, a sparsely furnished detention camp in Cuba, without trial and subject to torture. Suspected as terrorists, the men were from Afghanistan, Saudi Arabia, Yemen, Pakistan, and other countries.

Because the country was in such shock, there was little outcry about the violations of human rights taking place at Guantanamo.

★ THE WEAPONIZING OF IMMIGRATION ★

Unlike all the ways it had been considered in the past, immigration was now considered a security issue above all else.

Borders became much more of a national security issue. Enormous resources were taken from other areas of government and put toward securing the southern border and deporting noncriminal immigrants.

President Bush approved increasing border patrols from ten thousand to twenty thousand in 2008. Everyone now had to show international travel documents—passports—when crossing by car or plane.

In the decade after 9/11, American immigration policy was transformed from a guiding principle into a weapon to fight terrorism.

This represented an abrupt change in one of America's greatest themes. After 9/11, the days of welcoming "your tired, your poor, your huddled masses yearning to breathe free" seemed to be over.

CHAPTER SIXTEEN

★ ★ ★

The Never-Ending Immigration Debate

Despite the constrictions after 9/11, the waves of American immigration continued. America remains a desired goal.

Attitudes toward immigration continue to be a mirror held up to our society, reflecting what we fear, admire, recoil from, or welcome. Today's immigrants have both passionate critics as well as passionate advocates, with both groups speaking louder than ever.

For critics, the newest immigrants have seemed unwilling or unable to assimilate into American society, too committed to keeping their foreign connections, too far removed from core American values. These are familiar complaints from the past, as are ones about newcomers taking jobs away from Americans and putting burdens on the educational, welfare, and health-care systems. The anti-immigrant side sees the large number of undocumented immigrants—currently totaling 11 million—to pose a threat to the basic structure of society, its economy, its rules of law, and its health and education systems.

Immigrant advocates, such as the American Immigration Council, point out that each new wave of immigrants has evoked fear and suspicion from Americans—including the children and grandchildren of earlier immigrants. The claim that each group would somehow not fit in and would remain wedded to their old, foreign ways is a claim that keeps getting proved wrong, as with the Germans, Irish, Chinese, and many other groups. Most historians of immigration argue that immigrants enrich the United States, providing valuable services and new ideas.

> "It is my firm belief that immigration is not something to fear. We don't have to wall ourselves off from those who may not look like us right now, or pray like we do, or have a different last name. Because being an American is about something more than that. What makes us Americans is our shared commitment to an ideal that all of us are created equal, all of us have a chance to make of our lives what we will. And every study shows

that whether it was the Irish, or the Poles, or the Germans, or the Italians, or the Chinese, or the Japanese, or the Mexicans, or the Kenyans— whoever showed up, over time, by a second generation, third generation, those kids are Americans." —*President Barack Obama, 2016*

Nine percent of American public school students are not native English speakers, which hinders their performance in school. The vast majority of them speak Spanish. But there are lots of other languages, including Chinese (Cantonese and Mandarin), Arabic, and Vietnamese. Most English language learners (ELLs) were born in the United States and are US citizens. California has the largest percentage of them, followed by Florida and New York. The growth of the ELL population has been greatest in other states where resettlement agencies have helped immigrants move—places like Arkansas, Kentucky, Tennessee, North Carolina, and South Carolina.

⭐ Children's Books Lagging Behind

Since 1994 the Cooperative Children's Book Center has been keeping track of children's books by people of color—specifically by blacks, Latinos, American Indians, and Asian Americans. They make up a combined 38 percent of the population, but only seven percent of published children's books were created by authors or illustrators of color. The percent is increasing in recent years— but still lagging.

★ MINI MELTING POTS ★

Immigrants are everywhere, but they're often attracted to more affordable, rundown neighborhoods, helping to revitalize them. There are many success stories around the country.

Since the 1970s, thanks to church groups and resettlement agencies, Boise, Idaho, has a proud history of settling displaced persons. By 2016, 1,300 of its 26,000 students were refugees from war-torn countries all over. According to a local junior high counselor in Boise, no matter where they're from, the students all "share the same narrative: 'We had to move away from where we were. Bad things were happening. We are trying to have a happy life. This is the good part of our lives.'"

Immigrant Story—Zahraa Naser

After her father was kidnapped from their home in Iraq and murdered, Zahraa Naser fled to Syria with her mother and her two sisters in 2006. They were relocated to Boise, Idaho, where she graduated from Boise High School and is studying nursing at Boise State University. She will never forget the kindness of her teachers. "I loved those teachers. They were always the nicest, and even after you went out of the ELL (English language learners) program, they would always help you." She made some American friends, but her strongest friendships are with other refugees who have been dislocated like her. Recently she started wearing a hijab, the Muslim head scarf, as is the custom for girls in her culture once they reach a certain age. She could tell some friends were put off. "I think most people, when they see me, because I'm wearing the head scarf and I'm Muslim, think that I am, like, a terrorist, but I'm not," she says. "I'm just the same as them. I'm not any different."

Central Ohio has resettled more than seventeen thousand refugees from the Democratic Republic of the Congo, Myanmar, Bhutan, and Somalia since 1983. Resentment from the established community is common, especially after a Somali student attacked pedestrians and was killed by the police in 2016. But officials continue to welcome the refugees because of their importance to the local economy. They work in the meat-packing industry, and as engineers, doctors, and small-business owners, spending billions in the area and paying $1.3 billion a year in taxes.

★ Immigrant Story—Ruhatijuru Sebatutsi

As a teen, Ruhatijuru Sebatutsi fled war in the Congo in central Africa. After years in a Rwandan refugee camp, he was relocated to the United States in 2015. Today he lives with his wife and their eight children in Columbus, Ohio. As a meat-cutter at a factory that produces products like bacon bits and sausage patties, he logs in as many hours as possible. "I am so lucky." Making money is the best part of his new life. "The kids can ask you for something, you cannot provide," he said. "But here you work, you take care of your problems, you do something for yourself."

At one point, Nashville, Tennessee, had the fastest growing immigrant population of any city in America—Kurdish, Somali, Burmese, and Sudanese. They followed in the path of earlier immigrants from China, India, and Mexico. All newcomers were aided by especially active human-rights organizations, helping them through challenges that included resistance and discrimination.

California has a welcoming attitude and accepts more refugees than any other state. Because of a concentration of resettlement agencies (the International Rescue Committee, Catholic Charities, Jewish Family Services, and the Alliance for African Assistance) and well-established immigrant communities, San Diego County admits more than any other region, taking in thousands each year. The largest groups have come from war-torn Iraq, Syria, and Afghanistan. Since 1975, the city of El Cajon has been taking in refugees and now has the largest population of Iraq War refugees in the world. Said one Iraqi refugee: "America saved my life. The United States is free . . . in culture, free in speech, free in education."

With more immigrants than any other state, California depends on them for its workforce. Close to 40 percent of the state's full-time workers are immigrants. Nearly all workers in some jobs—sewing machine operators, agricultural workers, housekeepers, and dishwashers—are immigrants. High-skill professions also rely heavily on immigrants—electrical engineers, medical scientists, dentists, and pharmacists. More than 10 percent of the state's computer programmers were born in China. More than one in five registered nurses were born in the Philippines. More than a quarter of the software engineers were born in India.

More than ten percent of the population of Trinity County, California, is Hmong. These are people from mountainous regions of Vietnam and other countries, often persecuted for their religion. Those who helped America during the Vietnam War started fleeing here after the fall of Saigon in 1975, finding tranquility in the rural lifestyle.

"Little Saigon" neighborhoods of Vietnamese Americans are all over, with the largest one in Orange County, California.

Koreatown in Los Angeles has the largest number of Koreans outside Korea.

About fifty thousand Cambodian refugees settled in Los Angeles County. Many went to work in the doughnut business, where earlier waves of Cambodian immigrants already had bought shops and found jobs.

★ New York City

New York City remains Immigrant Central. It continues to absorb more newcomers than any other city, flourishing as an amazing zone of culture, the ultimate symbol for all that immigrants contribute. Following traditions established with Ellis Island, arrivals find plenty of job opportunities and family members already living there. More than a third of New Yorkers are foreign-born, and as many as eight hundred languages are spoken there. The borough of Queens, in particular, has more languages than anywhere in the world—Chinese (Mandarin and Cantonese), Greek, Filipino, Urdu, Indonesian, Russian, Japanese, Lithuanian, and others, including lesser-known ones like Chavacano, Waray-Waray, Minangkabau, and Bukharian.

The 1990s civil war in Somalia drove at least a million Somalis to seek asylum elsewhere. Some twenty-five thousand headed to Minneapolis–Saint Paul, where Somali immigrants had been going to school and working since the 1980s. Those who were already established helped the newcomers get jobs in meat-packing plants and open businesses of all kinds. That area now has the nation's largest Somali population.

★ PLAYING BY THE RULES ★

For almost its first hundred years, the United States had a system that allowed in any able-bodied immigrant. Back then, the biggest obstacle immigrants faced was just getting here—a costly journey full of danger—with some even selling themselves into indentured servitude to do so.

Today many rules specify who may enter and remain in the country legally.

A United States lawful permanent residency card is known as a green card because these identification cards, which started to be issued in 1946, were green. It is given to those authorized to live and work in the United States permanently, but without all the rights of citizens, such as being able to vote. To get a green card, immigrants usually have to go through a process that includes much paperwork to prove they are eligible, as well as filling out forms and being interviewed, a process that can take several years because of long waiting lists.

★ Millionaires Welcome

Any foreigner who invests between $500,000 and $1 million here, and creates at least ten domestic jobs from that investment within two years, is eligible for a green card.

There's also a lottery. Each year, some fifty thousand immigrant visas are randomly made available through the Diversity Visa program, also known as the Green Card Lottery. This applies to people born in countries with few immigrants to the United States for various reasons. These countries include Ethiopia, the Congo, Cambodia, Uzbekistan, and many others.

After five years of residency (three if married to an American citizen), a legal permanent resident can apply for citizenship. Applicants have to be able to demonstrate "good moral character." Serious crimes (murder, drug trafficking, assault, burglary) make a person permanently ineligible for becoming a citizen—they are likely to be deported. Some less severe crimes—such as shoplifting or disorderly conduct—can make a green card holder wait an additional five years to apply for citizenship.

Those who apply for citizenship have to take a test in

basic English skills and a test on their knowledge of the American government.

⭐ Could YOU Pass the Citizenship Test?

SAMPLE QUESTIONS:

- Why does the flag have fifty stars?
- What are the two major political parties in the United States?
- What are the two parts of the US Congress?
- The idea of self-government is in the first three words of the Constitution. What are these words?
- What do we call the first ten amendments to the Constitution?
- What stops one branch of government from becoming too powerful?
- Who is one of your state's US senators now?
- What are two cabinet-level positions?
- What are two rights of everyone living in the United States?
- What is one reason colonists came to America?
- What movement tried to end racial discrimination?
- Name one American Indian tribe in the United States.

Most of the foreign-born people living in the United States have gone through the process to attain permission to be here. Of the more than forty-four million foreign-born people who were living in the United States in 2018, around 44 percent were US citizens. Another 27 percent were lawful permanent residents, or green-card holders.

With nearly thirteen million migrants, Mexico takes the top spot for origin countries. After that, southeast Asia dominates: China (2.2 million), India (2 million), and the Philippines (2 million). Today, the majority of the country's immigrants hail from Asia and Latin America. Airports are the prime entry points—the ones in New York City, then Miami and Los Angeles.

Currently, there's no way to become a citizen unless you're a permanent resident first. Most undocumented immigrants don't qualify for green cards because of their lack of proper papers, and even if they do, the wait can be decades long.

★ President George W. Bush

A path to citizenship for the undocumented was first proposed by George W. Bush in 2006. "Their search for a better life is one of the most basic desires of human beings." It would have been a lengthy, difficult process. "What I have just described is not amnesty—it is a way for those who have broken the law to pay their debt to society and demonstrate the character that

President George W. Bush

makes a good citizen." Congress refused to act on establishing a path to citizenship and continues to do so, even though a CNN poll in 2010 showed that 81 percent of Americans were in favor of it.

★ Anti-Immigrant

"Citizenship is the greatest honor our country can bestow. It shouldn't be sold to lawbreakers for the price of a fine."—*Representative Lamar Smith of Texas*

★ THE PUSH-PULL OF THE OBAMA YEARS ★

When President Barack Obama took office in 2009, he made immigration a top concern, just as it was becoming for many Americans.

President Barack Obama delivers a speech.

⭐ Fixing the Broken System

"We can no longer wait to fix our broken
immigration system . . . [the path] must require
those who are here illegally to get right with
the law, pay penalties and taxes, learn English,
pass criminal background checks and admit
responsibility before they are allowed to get in line
and eventually earn citizenship."
—*President Barack Obama, 2010*

He too proposed a path to citizenship, but it failed
amid intense opposition from Congress. So he went on to
at least try to help young people, as we have so often done
in our immigration history.

Back in 2001, the DREAM Act had been proposed in the Senate—Development, Relief, and Education for Alien Minors Act. It would have put undocumented children on a path to citizenship, helping those who had been living here illegally because of their parents' move. Various versions of the act had been proposed, but it had never been able to pass in both houses of Congress.

Not Aliens

Illegal alien has been a term often used in the past, but many complain that it's negative and dehumanizing. In 2016 the Library of Congress, which creates subject headings for all books, threw out the subject heading *illegal aliens*. Preferred terms now are *undocumented workers, noncitizens,* and *unauthorized immigration*.

Obama tried to revive the DREAM Act in 2010. It would have granted legal status to millions of people between the ages of twelve and thirty-five, and a poll showed that 68 percent of Americans favored it. Said Obama: "They are Americans in their heart, in their minds, in every single way but one: on paper."

The act passed in the House, but failed in the Senate, so its future is in doubt. But in the meantime, the 2.1 million young people it would help—known as

Dreamers—became a powerful political force, activists fighting for change.

⭐ Immigrant Story—Indira Islas

Indira Islas fled gang violence in Mexico for the United States at age six with her parents (both doctors) and two younger sisters. In Gainesville, Georgia, her mother cleaned houses and her father worked in construction. Her parents stressed education, and she spent her free time reading the Magic Tree House series and other books. By middle school, every straight-A report card meant she could take a celebratory school trip. "They rewarded us by taking us skating or bowling," she says. "I felt like I was so smart, just getting the chance to go out for the whole school day with friends. That's when I said: 'I can make it.'" Islas began to throw herself into sports and volunteering. When she was in high school, under the Deferred Action for Childhood Arrivals (DACA) program, she was able to get a driver's license and a job at a supermarket. She was able to pay her own expenses, including braces for her teeth. Being able to work and drive legally and fit in with her classmates, Islas says, was "living the American dream." Although she was eager to go to college, Islas could find no path to do so until a friend told her about an organization called TheDream.US, which was offering college scholarships to undocumented students. Only seventy-six students would be chosen—and she was one. She went on to Delaware State University, studying to become a doctor.

The Dreamer movement was able to press Obama to take executive action in 2012 and pass the Deferred Action for Childhood Arrivals program, known as DACA. This grants limited deportation reprieve to some undocumented young people who came to the country as children. If they register with the government and go to college, they receive a two-year renewable protection against deportation, as well as work permits and Social Security numbers that allow them to hold jobs. As a way of helping them through college, they are eligible to pay in-state tuition rates at public colleges and universities— the same as what local residents pay.

The DACA program is popular—in 2018, 76 percent of voters believed the young people should be allowed to stay in this country. Even those who take a hard line against immigrants seem to find a soft spot for those targeted through no fault of their own—part of our long tradition of looking out for young people.

⭐ Immigrant Story—John Lennon

John Lennon, famed member of the Beatles, moved permanently from England to New York in 1971. President Richard Nixon, afraid that Lennon's anti-Vietnam war activism was going to hurt his chances for reelection, tried to have him deported. It took over three years of deportation hearings before Lennon's lawyers were able to win his battle (Lennon v. Immigration and Naturalization Service, 1975) and he received his green card certifying his permanent residency. Immigration laws, said one of his lawyers, are "like a magic mirror, reflecting the fears and concerns of past congresses." But the victory proved that people with sympathetic cases could be protected from deportation. Lennon was murdered in 1980, but in 2012, the Obama administration used his case as a precedent to set up the DACA program. "All I can say is, John Lennon is smiling in his grave," said a lawyer. "He helped accomplish that."

Obama once visited a Baltimore mosque and reminded the public that "we're one American family, and when any part of our family starts to feel separate . . . It's a challenge to our values."

At the same time, Obama greatly expanded the US

deportation machine, overseeing a higher number of border patrols than ever before. His administration deported 2.7 million people, more than any previous administration. It focused on repeat immigration violators and people with multiple criminal violations. But in 2013 it also deported 72,410 foreign-born parents whose children had been born in the United States. In some cases, this broke up families, as some of the children, under the DACA program, were allowed to stay.

The administration also deliberately deported children. The 2014 Central American refugee crisis, with tens of thousands of women and children (many of them unaccompanied) fleeing extreme violence, was considered one of the greatest refugee crises in history. Responding to political pressure, the administration's main response was to work on sending them back as soon as possible and to focus on intercepting and returning children en route. Obama met with the presidents of Guatemala, El Salvador, and Honduras to seek their cooperation in reducing the migration of children and speeding up their returns. He sent them large aid packages to help them permanently stem the flow.

The Syrian refugee crisis, with Muslim Syrians fleeing their bloody civil war, began in 2011, during Obama's administration. According to the United Nations, more than thirteen million Syrians needed humanitarian help.

The administration set a limit of ten thousand Syrians to admit and resettle. Even that number was controversial, with some thirty states fearing terrorists and refusing to admit any Syrians.

★ The Vetting Process

Resettlement agencies say refugees go through an extensive screening process that thwarts terrorists, with several additional layers of security screening and vetting including in-depth interviews and home-country reference checks. According to the State Department, no traveler to the United States is subject to more rigorous security screening than refugees. Over a period of forty years (1975 to 2015), of the 3.25 million refugees who came to America, a total of twenty have been convicted of planning or committing an act of terrorism on U.S. soil.

Also during Obama's administration, Haitian immigrants lost permission to stay here, which they had received after their country's devastating 2010 earthquake. In 2016, Haitians arriving at ports of entry were placed in detention centers and sent home unless they proved they feared returning because of political or religious persecution. Mexican residents, especially in Tijuana, took a more humanitarian approach. They received the Haitians with open arms, with officials offering documents that gave them formal permission to be in the country while they waited their turn to appear before US Customs and Border Protection.

Obama, the US commander in chief, came to be known in some circles as the "deporter in chief."

★ ENTER TRUMP ★

Businessman Donald Trump started his entire political career in 2011 with an immigration concern. He questioned whether President Obama had been born in America (he was—he was born in Hawaii). If Obama had been born in an African country, it would have made him ineligible to be the president, according to the Constitution. Trump promoted the so-called "birther movement" that attacked Obama's legitimacy in an overtly racist way.

Elected president in 2016, Trump continued to make immigration a major focus. The suspicion of immigrants as threats to society has always been close to the surface. Trump drew it back to center stage. In his words, "We only want to admit those into our country who will support our country and love deeply our people."

In his first month in office, he rapidly issued numerous orders affecting immigration policy. He lowered the number of refugees to be admitted into the United

States to forty-five thousand (compared to the previous year's 110,000—in 2019 refugees were capped at thirty thousand), and he suspended the entry of Syrian refugees indefinitely, calling for the deportation of those already here.

Syrian Refugees

Some eighteen thousand Syrian civil war refugees have settled in the United States since 2011, joining the ninety thousand Syrian Americans who have been here for years. The vetting process for them is lengthy and extreme, more so than for other groups. Said one woman about the years it took her family to enter: "I believe the screening we underwent was so intense, so thorough and

Former USAID Assistant Administrator Nancy Lindborg Interacts With Syrian Refugees in Turkey on January 24, 2013.

so long that it would be impossible for militants to come here. . . . My biggest dream is for [my daughters] to have a good education and good careers, and for us to be part of this society: to learn the language, to do something productive, to integrate."

Statement on Refugees Taken Down from the US State Department Site after the 2016 election

"The US Refugee Admissions Program embodies the United States' values of compassion, generosity, and leadership in serving vulnerable populations. The United States is the largest refugee resettlement country in the world, having welcomed more than three million refugees since 1975, helping them build new lives in all fifty states. The US Refugee Admissions Program has brought to the United States 70,000 of the world's most vulnerable refugees in each of the past three years, and plans to increase that number to 85,000 in 2016 and 100,000 in 2017. These refugees have added an immeasurable amount to the richness of American culture, contributed to our economic strength and honored our core values as a nation, engraved in our Statute of Liberty . . . Cities around the United States have benefited from the presence of refugees and immigrants."

Also in January 2017, building on the anti-Muslim prejudice after 9/11, Trump issued an executive order called "Protecting the Nation from Foreign Terrorist Entry into the United States." This was a travel ban on people coming here from seven Muslim-majority nations: Iran, Iraq, Libya, Somalia, Sudan, Syria, and Yemen.

President Donald Trump.

"In order to protect Americans, the United States must ensure that those admitted to this country do not bear hostile attitudes toward it and its founding principles. The United States cannot, and should not, admit those who do not support the Constitution, or those who would place violent ideologies over American law."

—*President Donald Trump, 2017*

Many were outraged at the discrimination, but there was precedent for Trump's executive order. It fit into a larger pattern of American history. Recall that back in 1882, out of racism and fear for American jobs, Congress banned Chinese immigrants from entering the US, and later almost all Japanese immigrants. The Chinese exclusion laws put into place the principles that could be used to justify discriminatory measures.

Later, in 1921, America gave preference to immigrants from Northern and Western Europe. Not until the Immigration and Nationality Act of 1965 did the government do away with national-origins quotas and ban discrimination based on where a person was from.

But once again, immigrants were being excluded based on origin from certain countries.

Some of Trump's advisors called publicly for immigration enforcement strategies so tough that they would encourage people to "self-deport," or leave on their own. Measures would include forbidding driver's licenses, cutting off access to social services and work opportunities, eliminating in-state college tuition, making a fake Social Security card a felony—a serious crime punishable by imprisonment in excess of one year. Others, including some police officers, see arresting immigrants as counterproductive, when law-abiding immigrants could help them solve crimes without fear of being arrested.

Trump's new orders represented a vast expansion of Obama's deportation policies. Included in the criminal category were large numbers of people who stated on employment forms that they were legally allowed to work. Trump's order called for targeting anyone who lied on their forms in order to get a job.

⭐ Immigrant Story—Wolf-Leib Glosser

Fleeing poverty and intense Jewish persecution in Russia, Wolf-Leib Glosser came to Ellis Island in 1903 with eight dollars in his pocket. He spoke no English. A son followed him here, and within three years, earning money as street peddlers and factory workers, they were able to pay for the rest of their family to come to America. During World War II, all but seven of the two thousand Jews who remained in their hometown were killed by Nazis. In America, the Glossers left poverty behind to become prosperous American citizens— merchants, scholars, and professionals. One of Glosser's descendants is Stephen Miller, who grew up in Malibu, California, and became a political activist, most notably the chief architect of Trump's restrictive immigration policies.

In the days after the Muslim travel ban, confusion abounded at airports. Hundreds were apprehended— including university students returning to the United States, holders of green cards and other valid visas, refugees, and employees returning to their jobs. Some were detained, others deported.

The chaos invited mistakes, as when Australia's best-loved children's author, Mem Fox, was detained at the Los Angeles airport. For two hours she was aggressively interrogated by immigration officials for traveling on the "wrong" kind of visa (which wasn't actually the case). Fox says she's unlikely to ever travel to the United States again after being made to feel like "a prisoner at Guantanamo Bay."

Trump went on to hint that he'd like to create a registry listing all Muslims already in the United States, as a way to monitor them. Very controversial, but again with a precedent in our history: the wartime rounding up of Japanese Americans. Trump had already suggested that he might have supported imprisoning people of Japanese ancestry during World War II.

One internment camp survivor reacted by saying, "It was all based on race hysteria, xenophobia in the past, and you don't want that to repeat again. But that's what's being encouraged at this point, and that's not what America stands for."

⭐ Irony

Regarding today's Muslim ban, surveys show that about 20 percent of Chinese Americans, and Asian American registered voters as a whole, support such a ban out of concern for national security—even though Chinese were the first in American history to be excluded because of their ethnicity.

Not a Melting Pot

"Then, things were a melting pot. You come here and you melt," said the head of a mosque in Iowa in 2017, referring to the early settlement of Muslims in America. "I'm very disappointed that Trump is signing executive orders like this so quickly without putting the necessary thought into what real impact it will have for our country, and for the refugees and others who look up to us as a bastion of hope and opportunity. This protectionist policy is bad for us and for our allies around the world. It is not what the majority of Americans want. I fear for the future."

Since Trump's Muslim ban, hate crimes against Muslims, or even those perceived to be Muslim, have increased. In February 2017, an Olathe, Kansas, man shot two men in bar, killing one, after reportedly telling them to "get out of my country." The shooter's comments implied that he thought they were of Middle Eastern descent. In fact, the men were aerospace engineers here on work visas from India.

Irony

Sikhs—followers of the East Indian religion of Sikhism—are frequent targets of those who confuse them with Muslims. All Sikh men wear turbans, as do some Muslim men. During one several-month period, more American Sikhs were shot by white American men than Americans have been shot by people from the seven banned countries in the past ten years.

Law enforcement agencies in the United States consider American anti-government extremists, not radicalized Muslims, to be the most severe threat of political violence that they face, according to the Triangle Center on Terrorism and Homeland Security.

A 2017 Department of Homeland Security report casts doubt on the need for Trump's travel ban. The report concludes that Middle Eastern citizenship is an "unreliable" threat indicator and that people from the banned countries have rarely been implicated in US-based terrorism.

Courts immediately challenged the legality of the ban, and it was blocked. In March, 2017, Trump issued a replacement ban, similar in intent, and courts challenged this as well. Courts differed on whether the president was acting in the interest of national security or out of religious discrimination. A US appeals court ruled it discriminatory, but in 2018 the Supreme Court ruled it constitutional and upheld the ban.

★ BORDER WALL ★

Trump launched his presidential campaign by accusing Mexico of sending its criminals to America. He called for a tall wall to be constructed along the entire border between the two countries, for this wall to be paid for by Mexico, and for a "deportation force" to deport those immigrants already here.

★ Deportation Numbers

Deporting all eleven million undocumented immigrants would mean arresting fifteen thousand people a day, seven days a week, 365 days a year for two years.

Trump's wall was also not a new idea. George W. Bush had signed off on the Secure Fence Act of 2006, approving a plan to keep Mexicans out as a step toward immigration reform. The act would have built seven hundred miles of fencing on the border, plus a virtual wall using high-tech equipment to patrol across the entire two-thousand-mile border. However, the war in Iraq was taking all of Bush's attention, and the wall plan was left behind. Neither Bush nor Trump mentioned the irony that the United States had seized this territory from Mexico in the 1840s, drawing up an arbitrary border.

⭐ Immigrant Story—Guadalupe García Aguilar

Guadalupe García Aguilar had been living in Arizona for twenty-two years, since she was fourteen years old (she had missed being eligible for DACA by just a few months). She was the mother of two American citizens, ages fourteen and sixteen. She once used a fake Social Security number to get a job at an amusement park. This was a felony crime, and when she was caught she spent three months in jail and three months in detention. She'd been able to remain in Arizona under what is known as an order of supervision, subject to routine check-ins. On her check-in on February 8, 2017, Aguilar became the first person deported under Trump's new executive orders on immigration. As she was taken into custody and put into a van in handcuffs, supporters chanted, "No está sola!" ("You are not alone!"). At a candlelight vigil that night, people protested. The police arrested seven people and dispersed the crowd, but by then Aguilar was already in Nogales, Mexico.

⭐ Irony

Mainly because of a lower cost of living, some Americans move or retire to Mexico. According to the United States State Department, almost a million Americans are living illegally in Mexico—without documents. In other words, 91 percent of Americans living in Mexico are "illegal." Mexican officials consider this a minor issue, and other than occasional small fines if they are caught, do little to target them.

According to 2018 polls, more Americans continue to oppose than favor a wall along the border with Mexico (62 percent to 35 percent).

Those opposed to the wall note the fact that undocumented immigrants are increasingly coming from Asia, Central America, and sub-Saharan Africa. So a wall along the border with Mexico would not stop them. History has shown that people, if they are truly motivated, have always found ways to cross walls and borders by air and sea as well as over land.

Until Congress passes a law that gives people a clear path to citizenship, undocumented workers, now more than ever, live with the anxiety of not knowing whether they will be able to stay in the United States. And the harsh new rules now have heightened this anxiety.

★ Immigrant Story—Larissa Martinez

In 2016, a Texas high school girl named Larissa Martinez graduated at the top of her class, awarded a full scholarship to Yale University. In her graduation speech she revealed for the first time that she had been living in the United States since age eleven as an undocumented immigrant from Mexico. "Immigrants," she told the crowd, "undocumented or otherwise, are people too." Her honesty earned her a standing ovation, and she went on to her freshman year at Yale living with the anxiety of possible deportation.

The tightening of immigration policy at the federal level has caused some to want to protect immigrants by offering sanctuary, or shelter from authorities. California and several other states passed laws declaring them "sanctuary states," stopping local and state law enforcement from using their resources to help federal immigration enforcement. In response, the federal government has threatened to cut off state funding for certain law-enforcement grants.

Churches across the country are establishing new sanctuary practices of their own. Freedom University, near Athens, Georgia, is a school for undocumented students shut out of the public universities, offering free college-level instruction. The school's exact location is secret, because Ku Klux Klansmen have threatened to break up classes and report students to authorities.

★ THE ZERO-TOLERANCE BORDER POLICY ★

Two weeks after Trump was inaugurated (on January 20, 2017), the administration started discussing the idea of separating immigrant children from their mothers as a brutal way to discourage asylum seekers. There was a new surge in families crossing the Mexican border—women and children fleeing gang violence in the Central American countries of El Salvador, Guatemala, and Honduras. Rather than crossing illegally, they were giving themselves up at the border hoping to claim asylum, something they are legally entitled to do.

In response, in 2018, Trump imposed the harshest immigration measure yet. He issued an executive order for a zero-tolerance border policy. In effect, this was a policy of family separation.

Unlike other times in history when America has helped children, federal authorities now had the power to physically separate children from their parents or other adults who had accompanied them. Adults were deported or prosecuted and sent to federal jails, while children and infants were placed under the supervision of the US Department of Health and Human Services. The policy led to the separation of thousands of children from their parents, according to government officials.

Zero tolerance border policy, detained children

Many individuals and organizations were horrified, condemning the policy as cruel and sure to cause trauma. Polls showed that only about 25 percent of Americans supported the policy. Trump later reversed it, and within a few months some 1,400 children had been reunited with their parents while seven hundred remained in government shelters. Officials are said to be working to return the remaining children, including those whose parents have already been deported without them.

★ THE FACTS ★

It is a fact that illegal immigration from Mexico has actually slowed way down over the past decades. The number of undocumented immigrants apprehended by the border patrol has been in steady decline.

As their own economy improves and the fear of deportation rises, more are leaving—deported or moving home—than are coming in, and this trend has accelerated since Trump took office. In recent years, the net inflow of new undocumented immigrants arriving from Mexico has fallen to zero.

★ Immigrant Story—Juan Manuel Montes

Juan Manuel Montes has lived in Calexico, California, with his family since he was nine. He has a cognitive disability due to a childhood brain injury. Twice he was granted protected status from deportation under Obama's DACA program. On February 19, 2017, then twenty-three, he was standing outside a restaurant, waiting for a ride home, when he was approached by Border Patrol agents. Montes did not have his wallet on him to prove that he was enrolled in DACA and said the agents refused to allow him to go pick up his identification. The agents deported him around 1:00 a.m. He is the first person with protected status under Obama's DACA program to be deported under Trump. Later that year, he sued the Trump administration over his deportation, but after six months, he dropped the case. He remains in Mexico, living with relatives.

As for the complaint that unauthorized immigrants don't pay the taxes that fund the American government—they do if they receive paychecks, from which various taxes are deducted, like social security tax. They pay sales, gasoline, and property taxes. Meanwhile they don't collect social security and don't qualify for food stamps or other benefit programs. The Social Security Administration estimates that unauthorized immigrants pay about $13 billion a year into social security and get only about $1 billion back. According to a 2017 study, refugees who entered the country as adults will have paid an average of $21,000 more in taxes than they received in benefits over their first twenty years in the United States.

★ Immigrant Story——Melania Trump

In then-Communist Yugoslavia, Melania Trump began her modeling career in 1986 as a teen, signing with a modeling agency that flew her to Italy. From there she went on to a successful career in New York on an H1-B visa, which allowed her to stay in the US for three years. She obtained a green card in 2001, making her a permanent resident, and became a US citizen in 2006, the year after marrying future president Donald Trump. "On July 28th, 2006, I was very proud to

Melania Trump meets with students in Kennedy Garden at her Be Best policy initiative rollout.

become a citizen of the United States—the greatest privilege on planet Earth. I cannot, or will not, take the freedoms this country offers for granted." In 2018 her parents also became citizens, by way of family-based sponsorship, or "chain migration"—a policy the president opposes.

Immigrants stimulate the American economy, producing a net benefit of about $50 billion since 1990. Farms and restaurants, hotels, manufacturers, retail businesses—all sectors of the economy benefit directly or indirectly from immigrant labor. Legal immigrants make up 5 percent of our active-duty military.

"Have you ever been to Arlington Cemetery? Go look at the graves of brave patriots who died defending the United States of America—you will see all faiths, genders, and ethnicities."

—*Khizr Khan, father of American army captain killed during the Iraq War*

Many studies show that immigration tends to raise productivity and increase economic output, mostly by multiplying the earnings of immigrants themselves.

★ Irony

Trump employs sixty-four foreigners at Mar-a-Lago, his resort in Palm Beach, Florida. They are mostly Haitians and Romanians here on H-2B visas, which allows employers to bring foreign nonagricultural workers here temporarily. At the same time, Trump supports a plan to cut legal immigration, including those on H-2B visas, by half.

Contrary to popular myth, studies show that immigrants do not push Americans out of jobs. Immigrants tend to fill jobs that Americans cannot or will not fill, mostly at the high and low ends of the skill spectrum. Immigrants from countries that outpace us in math and science are disproportionately represented in such high-skilled fields as medicine, physics, and computer science.

Immigrants with manual-labor skills need jobs that many Americans don't want to apply for, so they're often found in hotels and restaurants, domestic service, construction, and light manufacturing.

Another plus to immigration is that it increases innovation, opening up new opportunities in all areas. Evidence suggests that countries with a larger variety of immigrants are richer, more productive, and more innovative. Regions that receive more immigrants grow faster.

According to polls, the public is actually moving in the opposite direction from Trump since he won the election in 2016. Nearly two-thirds of Americans say they'd like to see a path to legal status for undocumented immigrants—especially the children—rather than deportations.

The future looks uncertain and confusing.

CHAPTER 17

★ ★ ★

The Future

The future of immigration in America may be cloudy, but a few things about it are still safe to predict:

+ People will always want to come here. In every era of US history, from colonial times in the seventeenth century through the early twenty-first century, women and men from around the world have opted for the American experience.

+ If people want to cross the border badly enough, they will find a way. It's human nature.

+ It's also human nature to be suspicious of people different from us.

- ✦ American immigration will never stop being a matter for debate.
- ✦ Advocates for immigrants will continue to call for an overhaul of US immigration laws to create a path to citizenship.

★ Toward the Future

"Sooner or later, immigration reform will get done. Congress is not going to be able to ignore America forever. It's not a matter of if, it's a matter of when. And I can say that with confidence because we've seen our history. We get these spasms of politics around immigration and fear-mongering, and then our traditions and our history and our better impulses kick in. That's how we all ended up here. Because I guarantee you, at some point, every one of us has somebody in our background who people didn't want coming here, and yet here we are."

—*President Barack Obama, 2016*

★ CHANGES TO COME ★

Because today's immigrants are largely people of color, the diversity of America is flourishing. Already, more nonwhite babies than white babies are being born.

By around 2040, experts say, whites are expected to be less than half of the nation's population. People of color will represent 57 percent of the population, and we will be a multiracial nation, with no single ethnic group being a majority. Multiracial people—those of two or more groups—make up an estimated 7 percent of Americans and they're predicted to grow to 20 percent by 2050.

Diversity, previously a hallmark of big cities, will continue to spread into suburbs and rural America. Immigrants have followed new jobs in agriculture and oil and natural gas production, and they've looked for more opportunity and cheaper housing. The tripling of the Latino and Asian American populations by 2050 will change the composition of communities across the nation.

Better education and an aging population will result in a decrease in the number of workers born in the United States who are willing or available to take low-paying jobs that require physical labor, like cleaning houses or picking fruits and vegetables.

Immigration is slowing the aging of the work force. By 2050, America will see a 42 percent growth in the working-age population. Since immigrants are generally younger and healthier than the native-born population, they strengthen the safety net for the aging population. A diverse workforce's ingenuity and productivity will sustain America's growth.

⭐ **Irony**

More people from Mexico—the largest source of low-skilled immigrant workers—are now leaving the United States than are coming in. As their own economy improves and becomes less reliant on agriculture and more on manufacturing, with rising wages, Mexicans are having fewer children and feeling less compelled to migrate north. Many American industries that employ a lot of low-skilled immigrant workers—such as agriculture, construction, and food services—are facing a potential shortage of labor. We will need new immigrants.

As minorities disperse from central cities and move to places that have less experience incorporating difference, backlash will continue. Some may feel a sense of displacement that comes from having lived for a long time in a community and seeing it change. They may get irritated by small things, like having to "press 1 for English," or seeing Spanish-language signs.

Diversity can cause people to withdraw from those who don't look like us, to pull ourselves in like turtles. Over the centuries America has come to terms with this knee-jerk reaction and has tended to move past it.

Now, more and more seem to be unable to. Hate

groups, already in the hundreds today, will probably continue to mushroom. Anger over Latino immigration and projections showing that whites will no longer be in the majority will drive them.

★ REFUGEES ★

Refugees will continue to flee here, aided by church groups, nonprofit resettlement agencies, and pro-immigrant organizations. Scan the headlines for stories about turmoil abroad—civil war, countries committing genocide or "ethnic cleansing," mass uprisings, dissidents imprisoned or executed. Those global hot spots are generating future waves of refugees. Because of the lag while they have to pass through security checks overseas, refugees will start coming from those conflicts several years afterward.

Human Beings

"Nobody is ever just a refugee [or immigrant]. Nobody is ever just a single thing. . . . Let us remember that the movement of human beings on earth is not new. Human history is a history of movement and mingling. Let us remember that we are not just bones and flesh. We are emotional beings. We all share a desire to be valued, a desire to matter. Let us remember that dignity is as important as food."—writer Chimamanda Ngozi Adichie, in observance of World Humanitarian Day

Also predicted is a new kind of refugee—environmental refugees from disasters wrought by climate change. Before the end of this century, more than a hundred million people are expected to face displacement from their homes by rising seas.

Much is written about climate change and the impact of rising seas on waterfront populations. But coasts are not the only places that will be affected.

Mexico City—the crowded capital city of Mexico, high in the mountains, in the center of the country—is a prime example. Rising temperatures are causing drought. More heat and drought mean more evaporation of precious water and yet more demand for water, adding pressure to tap distant reservoirs at huge costs or further drain underground aquifers, which could lead to the city's collapse by 2050. One study predicts that 10 percent of Mexicans age fifteen to sixty-five could eventually try to move north, potentially heightening already extreme tensions over immigration. By that time, according to another study, there may be more than 700 million climate refugees on the move.

⭐ Pro and Con

"Every government in the world has the obligation to decide what immigration number is right for the community in its care. My greatest concern is how the number that is chosen will affect our grandchildren's grandchildren. Will we condemn them to be packed in a highly regimented country approaching a billion people? Or will we make it possible for them to enjoy the qualities of life we today hold the most dear?"

—Roy Beck, founder of NumbersUSA, an organization trying to reduce immigration

"We always gain from immigration. History shows immigration has always been good for America."

—Dr. Pedro Noguera, urban sociologist

"It's the land of immigrants, who come here to be free. If nobody comes here, it's not the land of the free."

—a twelfth-grader, 2017

★ IMMIGRATION BENEFITS ★

If we can maintain our multicultural perspective, cultural innovation will continue. Already immigrants and their children are overrepresented in a broad range of achievements, including Nobel Prize winners, leading scientists, and top performing and creative artists. They have helped define American culture through literature, music, and art.

Immigrant children tend to do well in school and

are overrepresented in various competitions—academic, mathematical, scientific, and musical. First- and second-generation Indian immigrant children have had particular success in the National Spelling Bee.

⭐ Immigrant Story—Mike Krieger

An immigrant from Brazil, Mike Krieger moved to California to attend Stanford University in 2004. He went on to cofound Instagram, the photo-sharing app. He deliberately eliminated most text from the app—he knew from growing up in Brazil that English text would hinder Instagram's use in most parts of the world. His profit was $100 million when he sold the company to Facebook, and he is now a philanthropist.

Immigrants are, by definition, bicultural, and sometimes multicultural. They can navigate multiple languages and understand how people from different backgrounds think and respond. People with such backgrounds can see more choices, possibilities, interpretations, and nuance than people who know only one culture.

About 25 percent of all doctors practicing or training in the United States are foreign-born. In some inner cities and most rural areas, the percentage is significantly higher.

Nowhere is the contribution of immigrants more visible than in the high-tech and other knowledge-based sectors. Immigrants hold a third of the patents issued to US residents.

★ Immigrant Story—Max Lechvin

From a Ukrainian Jewish family, Max Lechvin moved to the United States at sixteen under political asylum and settled in Chicago in 1991. He went on to become cofounder of PayPal, Yelp, and other companies. In 2002, he was named one of the top one hundred innovators in the world under the age of thirty-five, as well as Innovator of the Year. He is a major contributor to FWD.us, an organization advocating immigration liberalization for highly skilled immigrants.

Silicon Valley, home to high-tech companies, would stop functioning if we closed our borders to skilled and educated immigrants. During one six-year span, more than two-fifths of the new companies in Silicon Valley had at least one founder from another country—from India, Russia, Britain, Iran, Canada, Israel, China, and elsewhere. They have created thousands of jobs and added billions of dollars to the American economy.

★ A New Museum?

Former Representative James P. Moran of Virginia, concerned about the number of ethnic museums on the National Mall in Washington, called for a National Museum of the American People. It would be dedicated to celebrating all immigrants, from our earliest days until now. "I do think there's merit in the idea of showing all the American people how all the various threads of ethnicities and races and religions came together."

★ CHANGING ATTITUDES ★

For more than twenty years, the Pew Research Center has been asking whether immigrants in the US "strengthen our country because of their hard work and talents," or whether they "are a burden on our country because they take our jobs, housing, and health care."

Opinions about immigrants have been shifting, perhaps because of an increase in tolerance as more and more of our population interacts with immigrants. In one recent survey, 59 percent of the public say immigrants strengthen the country, while 33 percent describe them as a burden. In 1994, opinions were nearly the reverse: 63 percent said immigrants were a burden and 31 percent said they strengthened the country. Currently, 81 percent of the public says that undocumented immigrants now living in the U.S. should be allowed to stay legally if certain requirements are met.

The number of H-1B visa applications, which are

reserved for foreign workers with specialized skills, has been showing a recent steep decline, according to the United States Citizenship and Immigration Services. Canada and western Europe are becoming much more open to scholars and researchers.

This worries many, including Microsoft founder Bill Gates: "America will find it infinitely more difficult to maintain its technological leadership if it shuts out the very people who are most able to help us compete."

From its experimental and underpopulated days during the American Revolution to its current status as an industrial world power, America has depended on immigrants.

In explaining the success of the American experiment, businessman Warren Buffett (the world's third-richest man) said, "You had a welcoming attitude toward immigrants who then did wonders for this country. . . . The quality of immigrants, the motivation of immigrants, this is what has contributed to the greatness of the country."

They arrived as foreigners—bearers of languages, cultures, and religions that may have seemed alien to America's essential core. Over time, they and their descendants built ethnic communities and at the same time participated in American life, contributing to the nation as a whole.

Khizr and Ghazala Khan, August 2016

Immigrant Story—Khizr Khan

Khizr Khan grew up in Pakistan, keenly aware of his country's lack of fundamental rights that are in the US Constitution. He and his wife immigrated to America in 1980 and later achieved citizenship. He became a distinguished lawyer, and he and his family were grateful for "the chance to avail ourselves of [America's] boundless promises of equality and freedom." One of their three sons became a captain in the US Army and was killed in Iraq, then awarded a Purple Heart and a Bronze Star. In 2016, Khizr made a speech honoring his son's sacrifice and stressing the importance of an inclusive America with liberty for all citizens. Khan is deeply passionate about raising awareness of the rights and protections that the Constitution provides for every American and calling attention to the symbol of hope it represents throughout the world. "[The Declaration of Independence] was our story, too. The story of Pakistan, the story of the subcontinent, the story, really, of all colonized peoples everywhere and in every era. This was my story and my parents' story and my grandparents' story before them. Except the Americans apparently had figured out a different ending than we had."

Even as the waves of immigration continue, there is reason for optimism. From colonial times to now, the newcomers have been resented, even hated—and yet all have assimilated. We have absorbed waves of immigration before and have not only survived but become stronger.

Our amazing founding documents, like the Constitution, limit the powers of government in order to reduce conflict and preserve individual freedom. The effect is to preserve diversity and tolerance in the United States of America.

America came from nothing to be what it is today because of immigrants.

SOURCES

★ ★ ★

The ACLU Immigrants' Rights Project, https://www.aclu.org/
   issues/immigrants-rights

American Immigration Council, https://www.
   americanimmigrationcouncil.org

American Immigration Lawyers Association, http://aila.org

Anbinder, Tyler. City of Dreams: The 400-Year Epic History of
   Immigrant New York. Boston: Houghton Mifflin, 2016.

Angel Island State Park, http://www.parks.ca.gov/?page_id=468

Barone, Michael. Shaping Our Nation: How Surges of Migration
   Transformed America and Its Politics. New York: Crown,
   2013.

Bausum, Ann. Denied, Detained, Deported: Stories From the
   Dark Side of American Immigration. Washington, DC:
   National Geographic, 2019.

Baynton, Douglas C. Defectives in the Land: Disability and
   Immigration in the Age of Eugenics. Chicago: University of
   Chicago Press, 2016.

Bayor, Ronald H. Encountering Ellis Island: How European
   Immigrants Entered America. Baltimore: Johns Hopkins
   University Press, 2014.

Bureau of Population, Refugees, and Migration, US State
   Department, https://www.state.gov/j/prm/index.htm

Californians for Population Stabilization, http://www.capsweb.
  org

Center for Immigration Studies, http://cis.org

Center for Migration Studies of New York, http://cmsny.org

Chinese American Museum, Los Angeles, http://camla.org

Chomsky, Aviva. "They Take Our Jobs!" and 20 Other Myths
  About Immigration. Boston: Beacon Press, 2007.

Chomsky, Aviva. Undocumented: How Immigration Became
  Illegal. Boston: Beacon Press, 2014.

Conservatives for Comprehensive Immigration Reform, http://
  immigrationreform.com

Council on American-Islamic Relations, https://www.cair.com

Daniels, Roger. American Immigration: A Student Companion.
  New York: Oxford University Press, 2001.

Daniels, Roger. Guarding the Golden Door: American
  Immigration Policy and Immigrants Since 1882. New York:
  Hill and Wang, 2004.

Define American, https://defineamerican.com

Ellis Island National Museum of Immigration, http://www.
  libertyellisfoundation.org/immigration-museum

FWD.us, https://www.fwd.us

Federation for American Immigration Reform, http://www.
  fairus.org

Freedman, Russell. Angel Island: Gateway to Gold Mountain.
  New York: Clarion, 2013.

General Society of Mayflower Descendants, https://www.
  themayflowersociety.org

Gerber, David A. American Immigration: A Very Short
  Introduction. New York: Oxford University Press, 2011.

Harrison, Geoffrey and Thomas F. Scott. New Americans.
  Chicago: Norwood House Press, 2014.

Hebrew Immigrant Aid Society, https://www.hias.org

Hoobler, Dorothy and Thomas. The German American Family Album. New York: Oxford University Press, 1996.

Hultgren, John. Border Walls Gone Green: Nature and Anti-Immigrant Politics in America. Minneapolis: University of Minnesota, 2015.

I Am an Immigrant Campaign, http://www.iamanimmigrant.com

Immigrants: We Get the Job Done Coalition, http://hispanicfederation.org/getthejobdone/

U.S. Immigration and Citizenship, https://www.usa.gov/immigration-and-citizenship

Immigration and Customs Enforcement (ICE), https://www.ice.gov

Iyer, Deepa. We Too Sing America: South Asian, Arab, Muslim, and Sikh Immigrants Shape Our Multiracial Future. New York: The New Press, 2015.

Japanese American National Museum, http://www.janm.org

Khan, Khizr. An American Family: A Memoir of Hope and Sacrifice. New York: Random, 2017.

Kuklin, Susan. We Are Here to Stay: Voices of Undocumented Young Adults. Somerville, MA: Candlewick, 2019.

Lohman, Sarah. Eight Flavors: The Untold Story of American Cuisine. New York: Simon & Schuster, 2016.

Marcovitz, Hal. How Should America Respond to Illegal Immigration? San Diego: ReferencePoint Press, 2011.

Migration Policy Institute, http://www.migrationpolicy.org

Museum of Chinese in America, http://www.mocanyc.org

National Immigrant Justice Center, immigrantjustice.org

National Immigration Forum, http://immigrationforum.org

National Immigration Law Center, https://www.nilc.org

The National Museum of the American People (proposed),
    https://buildnmap.com

New Americans Museum, http://www.newamericansmuseum.org

The New York Immigration Coalition, http://www.thenyic.org

NumbersUSA, https://www.numbersusa.com

Osborne, Linda Barrett. This Land Is Your Land: The History of
    American Immigration. New York: Abrams, 2016.

Pew Research Center, http://www.pewresearch.org

Progressives for Immigration Reform, http://
    progressivesforimmigrationreform.org

South Asian Americans Leading Together (SAALT),

The Statue of Liberty, https://www.nps.gov/stli/index.htm

Student Immigration Movement, http://simforus.org

Swain, Gwenyth. Hope and Tears: Ellis Island Voices.
    Honesdale, PA: Calkins Creek, 2012.

Tenement Museum, http://tenement.org

TheDream.US, http://www.thedream.us

United We Dream,

Wallace, Sandra Neil and Rich. First Generation: 36 Trailblazing
    Immigrants and Refugees Who Make America Great. New
    York: Little, Brown, 2018.

Wertheimer, Barbara Mayer. We Were There: The Story of
    Working Women in America. New York: Pantheon Books,
    1977.

PHOTO CREDITS

★⭐★

[TK]

INDEX

[TK]

ACKNOWLEDGMENTS

[TK]

TIMELINE

[TK]